INGER MEWBURN is a researcher who has specialised in research education since 2006. A former lecturer in architecture, she is currently the Director of Research Training at the Australian National University and creator of the popular blog *The Thesis Whisperer* (thesiswhisperer. com), which gives advice to PhD students. In addition to her journal publications and published papers, she is the author of the book *How to Tame Your PhD* (2013).

INGER MEWBURN

How to be an
ACADEMIC

THE
THESIS
WHISPERER
REVEALS ALL

NEWSOUTH

A NewSouth book

Published by
NewSouth Publishing
University of New South Wales Press Ltd
University of New South Wales
Sydney NSW 2052
AUSTRALIA
newsouthpublishing.com

© Inger Mewburn 2017
First published 2017

10 9 8 7 6 5 4 3 2 1

National Library of Australia
Cataloguing-in-Publication entry
Title: How to be an Academic: The Thesis Whisperer reveals all / Inger Mewburn.
ISBN: 9781742235073 (paperback)
     9781742244006 (ebook)
     9781742248387 (ePDF)
Notes: Includes bibliographical references and index.
Subjects: Universities and colleges – Faculty.
  College teachers – Employment.
  College teachers – Social conditions.
  College teachers – Political activity.
  College teaching – Vocational guidance.
  Dissertations, Academic – Authorship.
  Academic writing.

Design Josephine Pajor-Markus
Cover design Luke Causby, Blue Cork
Printer Griffin Press

CONTENTS

ACKNOWLEDGMENTS

I want to thank my team and colleagues at the Australian National University for being the very opposite of bad boyfriends, one and all. In particular I'd like to thank Professors Margaret Harding, Marnie Hughes-Warrington and Brian Schmidt, who have always been encouraging and supportive managers. Thanks to my PhD students, who have taught me more about how to be a research supervisor than any of the hundreds of papers I have read. I owe much to the late Robin Usher, who gave me a chance to prove myself, and would like to say a special thank you to Diane Mulcahy, for teaching me what academic generosity really looks like in practice.

Without amazing colleague friends, the Academic Hunger Games would be unbearable. Special thank you, in no particular order, to: Victoria Firth-Smith, Pat Thompson, Jason Downs, Scott Mayson, Sarah Stow, Tseen Khoo, Jonathan O'Donnell, Katie Freund, Ben Kraal, Xan Hordern, Lindy Burton, Glenda Amayo Caldwell, Evonne Miller, Geraldine Donoghue and all the members of Academic Fat Club, Mary-Helen Ward,

Sandra West, Megan McPherson, Narelle Lemon, Deborah Lupton, Deb Verhoven, Tamson Pietsch, John Ting, Julie Weymouth, Colleen Boyle, Lily Matthews, James Thompson, Nick Hill, Cathy Ayers, Sophie Lewis and Susan Mayson. Thanks also to Hannah Forsyth for introducing me to the wonderful New South people and to Will Grant and Hanna Suominen, for being great research collaborators. Special mention to Simon French for the Bad Boyfriend analogy. Extra special thanks to Ellen Speath for that conversation in that coffee shop in Glasgow (you are the reason I didn't abandon this book halfway through). Thank you to the rest of my #circleofniceness online, all over the world, especially Nigel Palmer and Rachael Pitt (the B-team), for always being willing to get your research education nerd on with me.

Thanks to my father, Roger Blackford, for instilling the love of learning and to my late mother, Velma, who is definitely responsible for that practical side everyone talks about. Since one of my nephews, Charlie, wanted me to mention him in the acknowledgments, I will give a big Aunty shout out to the rest of my nieces and nephews as well: Abi, Rose, Bennet, Gus, Oliver, Flynn and a yet to arrive niece (who we are all looking forward to meeting). Please study hard. Biggest thanks to Anitra Nottingham, best twin-sister ever, for always being there and willing to listen to me whinge – and for marrying Mark Nottingham, who persuaded me it was a good idea to blog.

This book would not have been possible without the loving support of Luke Mewburn, husband, friend and feminist accomplice. Thank you for being the best boyfriend a girl could ever want. Big love to my son Brendan Mewburn, for patiently enduring a mother who has a life of 'endless homework' and embarrasses you at parent–teacher nights. I love you more than I can ever express. This book is for both of you.

INTRODUCTION: THE ACADEMIC HUNGER GAMES

I write best when I am angry. I wish it were otherwise, but there you are. Luckily, my anger has a productive outlet.

My blog, *The Thesis Whisperer*, is dedicated to helping PhD students everywhere. It's a local newspaper for PhD students. A place where they can read stories about what's happening in their community, some of them written by other students. PhD students have to do a lot of reading, so the blog offers concise posts, every Wednesday morning, on topics that will interest them. It's not a 'how to' guide for doing a thesis, but it regularly offers practical tips and techniques that might help. There are a lot of posts on writing – a bugbear for many students – but there's a lot more to getting a PhD than writing a dissertation. So the blog features stories on communicating, workplace productivity and employability, among other, more marginal concerns such as whether or not you should include a glossary or what to wear to give a conference keynote. The primary purpose of the blog, though, is to stimulate conversations, which is why I am so delighted that half the posts are written by the community. When I was a PhD student I used to think that life after the PhD would be different somehow. I quickly realised that being a full-time academic was just more of the same. The uncertainty, annoyances and frustrations of the PhD are still there, minus, of course, the looming deadline of examination. I think this is why my blog has always appealed to practising academics as much as to PhD students.

I am often complimented on my sense of humour and the light touch with which I treat serious subjects, so regular readers might be surprised to hear that so much of my writing is driven by a deep sense of anger. I'm angry at the injustice I see in our contemporary university workplaces; I suppose humour is my way of coping. The other way I cope is to use my skills as a researcher to inform my blogging work, because knowledge is power.

When common problems are not discussed openly in a community, they tend to fester. This is why the blog features stories about doing the PhD written by students. Knowing that other people experience the same difficulties with the PhD is critical to success. If you start to struggle, it's not necessarily your fault. You are not inadequate or somehow defective, just part of a system that has built-in problems and challenges. You can stop telling yourself 'I'm not good enough' and start asking more important questions, like 'Why do I feel this way and what can I do about it?'.

The blog is my way of giving back, of supporting the newest entrants to our academic community, our amazing PhD students. The ultimate aim of teaching is to help people realise their potential and move on to the next stage of their life, whatever that might be. I feel privileged to have worked for the last ten years in an area of education where the expectation is that your students will become your future colleagues. Close friendships between supervisors and students are quite common. Some people go on to collaborate for decades when the PhD is over.

It's both humbling and fascinating to work with PhD students. They are a motley crew in some ways. Similarly to most places in the world, the average age on entry to a PhD in Australia is 32 and we have students at my university from 23 to 82. When working with such a diverse student population you are not really a teacher in the conventional sense. I'm a combination of coach, sounding board and advisor – and the blog reflects this. To students, my knowledge base can make me seem magical, even though it's just the result of a lot of reading, listening and time. It's rare that I encounter a PhD student problem I haven't seen before and I have a vast repertoire of possible solutions and strategies drawn from my reading of the literature generated by other research education academics. I'm deeply committed to helping our best and brightest students through this often gruelling academic rite of passage.

Over the years the blog has steadily gathered more readers. At time of writing there are around 80 000 people who follow *The Thesis Whisperer*, either by email or on one of my many social media channels. I am the poster girl for the benefits of academic blogging. My career has blossomed as a result of all this free work. Blogging has never really fitted into my work week. Like many other academics, my schedule is filled to the brim with meetings, teaching and other commitments. I edit reader contributions and write my own blog posts on quiet Sunday afternoons. I don't want to be part of promoting the culture of overwork in the academy, but I honestly enjoy this time. I consider the blog a form of public service as well as a creative outlet. I love to curl up with a cup of coffee and my laptop on the couch, read guest contributions, edit, write correspondence and ... angry posts.

――――――

I work in an area of education that most people don't know much about. Most people enter a PhD expecting to become an academic, but in many countries there simply aren't enough jobs to allow everyone to achieve their academic dream. PhD students are often being advised by people who never experienced the kinds of struggles in getting a job that exist now. In the last 30 years the structure of the workforce has changed beyond recognition. So many academics are on extremely short-term contracts, sometimes for years on end, struggling to pay the rent while doing what they love. They are more like fruit pickers than conventional office workers – most of the work on offer is seasonal and there can be long dry spells between contracts. The Academic Hunger Games can be brutal. I spent some 11 years working as a 'casual academic', when I felt anything but casual about my work. I only managed to survive financially with the help of my spouse, the ever-supportive Mr Thesis Whisperer. I've managed to hang in there long enough to achieve the status of associate professor at a prestigious research university, but even now I'm on a contract. I'm part of that generation who have never known an academia that is not precarious.

Maybe that's why I feel more like the survivor of a plane crash than a success story.

At the start of 2013 I self-published a book of blog posts, *How to Tame Your PhD*, containing my best posts on doing a dissertation, for the price of a coffee. It's sold thousands of copies and the profits have been put towards the cost of running the blog. I've had many offers over the years to write a 'proper book', but those publishers wanted new material. I'm grateful to New-South Publishing for being brave enough to go with my vision of blog-to-book. NewSouth were not afraid of the fact that a lot of this material is available online for free. They understand that books offer a convenient format for digesting blog posts and – importantly – you can finish reading a book! This book is a compendium of what I consider to be my best material about academic life and how to survive it. Putting the book together gave me the opportunity to edit, revise and sometimes rethink my original posts. This is the better version – Thesis Whisperer 2.0, if you like. The only way to learn to be an academic is to fumble your way through it, but other people's stories can be helpful. This book documents my thoughts, ideas and approaches to being an academic in the 21st century, written with full recognition that there is no one perfect way to have an academic career.

The impetus for putting together this book was another academic's story – Richard Hil's *Whackademia: An insider's account of the troubled university*, coincidentally by the same publisher. You've got to admit Hil nailed the title. Academia is whacky. I've sold stuff in supermarkets and book stores, dabbled in the music industry, washed dishes in restaurants, driven courier trucks and cleaned houses. Before I started working full-time in universities I spent nearly a decade working in architecture offices (believe me when I say these are strange places), but academia is, without doubt, the weirdest place I have ever worked.

But Hil's version of academia made me angry. I was angry when I agreed with what he had to say, but even angrier when I disagreed. When I put the book down I was deeply conflicted. So much of it was a spot-on critique of the contemporary Australian university system, but in my view it fell short of its aim of being a resistance manual for the contemporary academic. Perhaps this is a generational thing. Unlike me, Hil had the good luck to go to university in the 1970s and didn't have to pay for his education. I started my undergraduate education in 1989, the year fees were introduced in Australia. I am a child of the system Hil described as a kind of golden age of higher education.

The 1980s and '90s didn't seem like much of a golden age to me, perhaps because I remember it as a student, not a staff member. Personally I am happy that our campuses are a bit more like shopping malls. Anyone who had the dubious distinction of dining in the RMIT cafe in 1989, which specialised in mashed potatoes that bore a startling resemblance to prison food, will agree with me. You certainly couldn't get a decent coffee on campus for love nor money. And it's not just the food that has improved. University staff might have worse working conditions, but students are certainly better off. I remember those 'golden years' as being full of boring, irrelevant lectures from professors who had not changed their slides since the 1960s.

The regulations, policies and quality measures – and the paperwork that goes with them, which many academics (including myself) find a tedious bore – are an essential part of managing a large and complex university system. I have the dubious pleasure of working in the most lightly regulated area of university teaching. Until recently, PhD degrees didn't even have time limits, let alone statements of outcomes and expectations. Working without much regulation creates problems for PhD students and for staff. Universities sell the opportunity to gain a degree, but some PhD students find all sorts of barriers are put in their way. I don't write much about the examples of poor supervision I've seen in my ten years working in research education, but that's not because I haven't encountered it. Most of the problems I see are due to a lack of oversight and rules, not because of them.

I do, however, agree with the central premise of Hil's *Whackademia*: that there are deep and troubling problems in our academic workplaces. The university is no longer a happy community of scholars living in an intellectual meritocracy – if indeed it ever was. My colleague Simon French says the contemporary university is like a bad boyfriend: happy to date you, but reluctant to commit to a long-term relationship. Casual work is easy to come by; a permanent position is much harder to obtain.

Some years ago a more senior academic gave me a little pep talk about the difference between nepotism and patronage and the importance of cultivating Contacts. It took a while to appreciate the value of this cold-blooded advice. I went on to be rejected four times before I had to face up to the sad truth: no architecture department was going to hire me. Just like a bad boyfriend, the university was not willing to commit. I was just not sexy or interesting enough. I didn't have a PhD or a list of publications the length of my arm. I needed to let go of my *Brideshead Revisited* fantasy of professors sitting around, drinking port with their students in book-lined rooms. It's an unhappy truth that a research-heavy CV is the tight leather trousers of the university employment dance. Teaching ability is like a good personality – no one is going to take you home from the disco. Simon French reckons some people lead a charmed life and don't get their heart broken until they fail to get promoted into the professoriate, or get retrenched because someone decides the university isn't teaching medieval history anymore. Some PhD students are broken early on by a research supervisor who makes their life a living hell. Simon talks about bouncing back after the university has become your bad boyfriend. It's true that people do react in different ways to being unlucky in love. Some will swear off having a relationship forever and go out to get paid more in the private sector; others stay, but are permanently bitter.

I don't like bitterness. I decided to continue to love the university, while being aware of its faults. I put on the tight leather trousers of the academic employment disco and got a PhD. Fast forward nearly 15 years and, although the permanent job eludes me still, my contract is so long I am not really worried. I've learned to live by my wits and survive the Academic Hunger Games on my own terms. While I liked where Hil was going with much of his critique, in my opinion the resistance tactics he offered at the end of his book were just not useful. Most of them were geared to making it hard for your managers. I think this is tilting at the wrong windmill. Overwhelmingly, managers are just trying to cope with a system that is fundamentally unmanageable and underfunded; the real problem is the lack of vision and investment by successive governments. Academics without the benefit of a permanent position (tenure) would probably find themselves without a job next year if they made their managers' lives hard by following Hil's resistance approach. This is fine for people with defined benefits superannuation who only have to survive a few years until retirement, but for the new scholar, it's career suicide.

So this book doesn't tell you how to resist; I seek

instead to empower. I want you to think about your own terms of engagement with the bad boyfriend university, either as a PhD student or an academic. I want to help you win the Academic Hunger Games, but not by stepping on other people's throats. I want this book to help you think about what kind of academic you want to be and what sort of workplace you want to help create for yourself and others.

————

Some of the posts in this book deal with the emotional sides of academic life; others reflect on the kind of behaviours which are common in academia – and how to deal with them. Still more offer lessons on dealing with academia as a workplace and the kind of skills needed to prosper there. Some include more than a little critique of academia itself.

Regular readers will recognise some posts, no doubt, but you could think of this book as the remixed, 12-inch extended edition of the original songs. Creating this book gave me a rare opportunity to pull together scattered bits of writing from the blog and other bits of journalism, such as magazine articles; it was a bit like fitting pieces of a jigsaw together. Sometimes I've taken a paragraph from one post and attached it to the end of another, or pushed two whole posts together and edited them to the point where it has become something entirely new.

Like many academics, I have certain obsessions: the town/gown riots in medieval universities, the social function of food in academic settings, and a love of verbs that sometimes frightens my students. I tend to return to the same themes again and again, so the chapters came together relatively easily. Each is about different ways of being an academic. I start by reflecting on the culture of academia and the people who inhabit it. I follow with a chapter on being productive, touching on the specific workplace challenges and how you can use technology to solve them. In the chapters on writing and productivity I include posts on making academic work faster and easier, so you don't get overwhelmed. My special interest as a researcher is employability, so in that chapter I have brought together posts that offer advice on how to win the Academic Hunger Games, as well as cautionary tales. The final chapter has been reserved for my most angry posts – those I have written for my union newspaper, reflecting on the broader political issues that impact academics and their work.

I'm not a cynic. I still believe in the university and its mission of teaching and research. As individual academics we need to find ways to preserve the things we care about in our work and our home life. One of the things we must guard against is too much dependency on our employers. It's quite clear to me that while individual managers care a great deal, the system itself is heartless. Cultivating independence is crucial. I will speak often about strategies that have worked for me, or that I have observed working for others. Along the way I hope to offer helpful ideas for managing the multiple, and often competing, demands of being an academic, while meeting the inevitable performance expectations which seem to disproportionately affect those at the bottom of the academic hierarchy. Throughout, I want to question the idea of the 'normal' academic.

Ever since I became a teacher, and more so since I started to blog, I have been consistently praised for being 'practical'. At first I was not sure how to take this praise – my ego would have much preferred 'interesting' or 'creative'. But being forever practical seems to be my fate. Lately I have decided to embrace my practicality (it's an underrated virtue in academia).

This book honours the blog post format. Although you can read it in a linear fashion, you can jump around as much as you want and it will still make sense. I like to think of it as a survival manual for those in the profession, or those who are about to enter it. In that spirit, I commend these posts to you and hope they help you, in some small fashion, become the kind of academic you want to be.

Stay angry, friends.

1

BECOMING 'THE THESIS WHISPERER'

I became an academic blogger, appropriately enough, over lunch (though my photoblog exploring the role of food in academia was still in the future).

This particular lunch was with my brother-in-law, Mark Nottingham. Mark was born in the United States, but my twin sister Anitra had dragged him to Australia to marry her some 20 years ago. I'd asked Mark to lunch to get some career advice for one important reason: he was successful, but he wasn't an academic.

Prior to this lunch I'd played the Academic Hunger Games for 11 years, doing a bewildering range of casual teaching jobs while I completed two postgraduate degrees and raised a child. A series of lucky breaks and sideways moves had led to a position doing professional development workshops for PhD students. Being a research educator was a strange job and I was unexpectedly good at it, but it was precarious. My contract was going to run out soon and I had no idea where the next job was coming from. Other academics told me 'Just publish and everything will be fine'. But while my list of research publications was longer than that of most people of my age and stage, I'd just had five unsuccessful job interviews in a row and my early career academic friends didn't seem to be benefitting from the 'publish-or-perish' advice any more than I was. Good people were passed over for job opportunities or had funding run out unexpectedly. Everything that was solid, as Karl Marx once said, could easily melt into air.

In the decade I'd been hanging around academia full-time, I'd seen many a person fall victim to a restructure and have to move interstate, or across the world, to secure a new position. The job market was brutal and seemed full of hidden rules that did not match the conventional advice. People with fewer publications on their resume were routinely appointed over those with lots of them. There was always a preferred candidate before each job was advertised, despite the outward appearance of fairness. In one case it was rumoured an influential professor didn't want to lose his research assistant when the 'soft money' ran out. (Some people have salaries funded entirely from grants. If the next project is not funded, these people will quickly find themselves unemployed.) In another case, an extremely well-qualified female candidate was passed over, it was said, because the Dean thought there were 'too many women' already. I'd come to the conclusion that the publish-or-perish advice was just a nice way of saying 'Play by our rules and do your time'.

I needed a fresh perspective and Mark seemed to have it. In the 20 years I've known him, Mark has worked in the tech industry. As is common in that industry, he has changed jobs frequently, but what has always impressed me is that he seems to do it with no visible anxiety. If Mark was bored or felt he was being treated badly, he would just quit – he once did this only weeks into a role. He has always been in hot demand, which is curious because to this day no one in the family is really sure what he does. All I knew at this point was that Mark was 'internet famous', which is a strange kind of invisible celebrity. There's a Wikipedia page about Mark and, if you look him up, you'll see he's clearly a thought leader in his field – but you've probably never heard of him. That's because internet fame is all about occupying a niche. Only a small number of people in each country care about what he does, but because they are all connected by the internet, his celebrity has critical mass.

By the time the main course of this lunch was served, I'd been talking for 20 minutes straight about everything that was wrong with my part-time sort-of-job and what sort of permanent academic job I wanted instead.

Mark looked confused. 'I'm hearing about where you work, Inger, but I still don't really know what you actually do.' This was nothing new. Even other academics didn't understand what I did for a living.

'I'm a research educator', I replied, as patiently as I could.

'Yes, but what do you do?' Mark repeated insistently.

'Um … research education stuff?'

Mark rubbed his forehead and took another sip of his wine. I pushed my salad around my plate as an uncomfortable family silence settled over the table. I glared at Anitra over the table. She was the one who had suggested taking Mark out to lunch in the first place.

Mark put down his wine and tried again. 'Yes, research education. OK. But what does that actually mean? Remember that I know nothing about academia.'

Mark has a degree in photojournalism, but had spent a long time retraining himself in all things internet. In his field, a Masters degree or PhD is common enough, but he didn't need one – he's good at what he does and everyone who matters knows it. I sighed and tried to explain myself. I told him I ran workshops for PhD students on stuff like writing, organising, job hunting, presenting and, well, the politics of academia. That I acted in an advisory role, interpreting the rules and processes of the university for PhD students and their supervisors. Supervisors and students were always getting angry at each other and fighting. Because of the unique position of research students – part staff, part junior colleague, part student – these are more like workplace disputes than standard academic problems. Fixing these problems requires a certain degree of rat cunning and a good grip on theories of power. I suppose you could say that part of my job at that time was a weird sort of workplace mediation. In what time I had left over, I wrote academic papers and did research about what makes for a successful PhD experience.

I took another gulp of wine, searching for a way to sum it all up. 'If academia was *Pulp Fiction*, I would be Mr Wolf, hosing down the scene of the murder and finding everyone a fresh change of clothes.'

My sister laughed. She had been listening to my stories about work for a couple of years now. Mark didn't laugh; he just looked at me, clearly still confused. 'I'm a kind of troubleshooter, a fixer …' I trailed off lamely. 'Actually, you know what? I'm not even sure what it is I do either, but they're happy to pay me, so I don't question it too much.'

———————

Explaining my job to other people, even other academics, was always frustrating. Research education and the development of PhD students hadn't started until after the turn of the century. When this lunch discussion took place, people like me had only been around for about ten years. Even other academics have trouble understanding how you can help a PhD student in astrophysics if you know nothing about deep space telemetry, but you can. Being a research educator requires a wide range of skills in writing, presenting, teaching and researching, but there's no course you can do. It's kind of a hidden profession, which probably explains why everyone who ends up in research education is a refugee from somewhere else. There's someone like me in every university, but the title will shift: learning advisor, academic consultant, academic skills specialist. 'Research fellow' is what they call you when they can't think of anything else.

I was a fairly typical example of this mongrel research educator breed. I started an architecture degree at RMIT University in 1989, but after two years of the five-year course I decided it wasn't for me. I dropped out, travelled, washed dishes and managed a record store before deciding to go back, mainly because I couldn't think of anything else to do. The break had been a good idea, in retrospect. When I came back to study I discovered I had a gift for computers, which were arcane and difficult to work with back then. The university had invested heavily in these machines, but the middle-aged, full-time tenured professors in the department were out of touch and didn't have a clue how to train people in this new technology. Bright students were recruited to fill the gap and thus began my very early introduction to university teaching.

The money from casual teaching was really good compared to dishwashing and I enjoyed untangling the mysteries of AutoCAD for first-year students. I managed to spend about ten years working full-time as an architect and teaching in the evenings just because I enjoyed it. Pity I couldn't say the same about architecture. The office culture in the building industry, as I experienced it in the 1990s, was hostile to women and a ridiculously unhealthy, exploitative workplace (and I have little reason to think it's changed substantially since I left). I spent five years drifting from office to office as a computer gun for hire. My last job in the profession was doing what I called 'architectural pornography': creating images of apartment towers for the marketing department of a large corporation. At a certain point I realised I was really working in advertising, not design. This hadn't been the plan, but the money was good.

Then my mother died.

It was the end of a long battle with cancer. My freelance lifestyle enabled me to spend long periods of time keeping her company at various treatments and sitting by her bed, talking. We disagreed about a lot of things, but there was a deep bond between us. Medical technology greatly protracted the process of dying. Most of the time she was relatively comfortable, but the mental anguish took its toll on the whole family. During those long bedtime vigils I had plenty of time to think about what I didn't want from life. When I returned to the business of architectural pornography I was on the slippery slope from boredom to depression. My husband Luke had noticed how much I enjoyed teaching and encouraged me to look for a job in academia.

At first academia seemed like heaven. I had no trouble finding steady work in the vocational education side of the business, teaching the rendering and animation skills I had honed in practice. I was willing to work nights and weekends and teach in a broad range of subjects. I was offered a permanent, full-time teaching role in a technical college and I would probably still be there now if Thesis Whisperer Jnr hadn't come along.

I struggled with the lack of sleep, but I struggled more with the expectations of contemporary motherhood and the academic workplace. I returned to work part-time and the passive-aggressive questioning began immediately – mostly, but not entirely, from the old white guys who still dominate many departments.

'Why are you leaving your baby in daycare?'

'What does your husband think of you working?'

'Why are you bringing your baby to work? If you want to be with him, stay home.'

'My wife stayed home with all our four children. She's an amazing mother.'

'How much money does your husband earn? Can't he support you?'

'There's yoghurt on your dress.'

I got the message. I had been bringing Brendan into the office before class so that I could spend a few more precious moments with him before I had to drop him at daycare. I stopped doing this and the hostile stares stopped, but I started to get angry at the lack of support. I stopped being a compliant employee. Weekends and nights were out. When I got sick I took sick leave instead of struggling in so the class wouldn't have to be cancelled. I complained about pointless meetings without agendas. I refused to do overtime or to come to exhibition openings after hours. I think the breaking point was when I walked out on 'entrepreneur training', protesting that I was there to be a teacher, not a business leader (an irony considering my later career moves). In short, I became The Problem of the Department, but they didn't want to sack me. Legally, they needed to show support for women coming back to work part-time after maternity leave, so I was simply presented with a schedule that was impossible to manage. I still remember the guilt on the department leader's face when I told him I couldn't afford full-time daycare on my part-time salary and had to resign. 'Oh well. You'll have more time with your baby', he said.

I'm sure this made him feel a lot better.

With nothing left to lose, I started a Masters degree by research when Brendan was eight months old. Returning to study was a revelation. I'd always been an erratic undergraduate, more interested in boys and booze than my work. As it turned out, the problem had been too much time. Writing a whole thesis during long toddler naps and on the weekend was my only option. Daycare days were expensive and reserved for when I had paid work. With less time to muck around and second-guess myself I was focussed and diligent.

The best part was I found out I wasn't alone. Around half of the research students I met had family responsibilities – either to a spouse, elderly parents, animals or children. We were all in the same boat, struggling with the casual academic gig economy and trying to make it work amid the chaos. I made lots of new academic friends in those years and initially the casual teaching lifestyle actually suited me – at least there were no passive-aggressive questions or disapproving old white guys. But balancing the available daycare time with classes was tricky. My income covered the daycare and study expenses, but that was it. By the time I took into account all my preparation time, I was earning about $17 an hour – the same amount I'd earned managing a record store ten years before. I was teaching up to 25 hours a week at four different universities, which was mentally taxing to say the least, especially on limited sleep. I started to resent my full-time colleagues with permanent academic jobs. According to my calculations, they were paid double what I was getting for half the work.

What I didn't realise was that my ease in getting casual work would not translate to full-time tenured employment. Just as a bad boyfriend will leave you standing out in the rain when he's promised to pick you up, the bad boyfriend university fundamentally does not care about you. It doesn't care about your career ambitions, or even if you can pay the rent. I had a liberating insight: loyalty to any academic employer is pointless. Good people always have lots of options. The university should be looking to take care of its good people, but it doesn't, and getting upset about it doesn't help anyone, least of all yourself.

I stopped thinking of myself as a second-class academic citizen and started to talk about myself as a gun for hire; I was open to anything that came my way. Finally I was the perfect dancing partner for the neo-liberal, bad boyfriend university who is happy to use you, but doesn't want to offer you security. Opportunities I didn't know existed came out of the woodwork. When the opportunity came up to do a six-week, part-time gig in research education I grabbed it. The contract was extended and then extended again. I decided to give up the casual design teaching and make myself more available for this new kind of work. Of course, a bad boyfriend is at his most charming when you tell him you want to leave. Unbeknownst to me, one of the departments I worked for had come to rely on me to fill vital gaps in their first-year schedule. When I told them I was unavailable they tried really hard to keep me for the first time, then got angry when I refused. I guess they thought I was always going to be an easy lay.

———————

After the first week of doing research education I had an inkling that I had finally found my calling. After the six weeks, I was sure. Research education was different from anything I had done before, but my skills and general aptitude seemed to be a perfect match for it. I was given a vague brief to run a couple of workshops for PhD students and left to my own devices. My design background, where you are taught to solve ill-defined and complex problems, proved to be an unusual advantage. I started to build classes I would have wanted to attend when I started my Masters degree. I read a lot of the research about academia as a workplace – a workplace that had long fascinated and annoyed me in almost equal measure. Students seemed to enjoy my approach, I think due to the fact that I was one of them – I had started my own PhD in 2006 – and understood how they felt. At the end of the contract a colleague said, 'Oh, just keep turning up. They'll find something for you to do and a way to pay you.'

I just kept turning up.

People found things for me to do.

I need to take a moment here to acknowledge my privilege. I'm white. I'm heterosexual, cisgendered and married. Yes, I have experienced discrimination and lived with the feeling that I don't really fit in, but I still had more resources than some others. My husband's 'precarious' private sector job income offset my lack of certainty in my 'secure' public sector job for nearly 12 years. It's because of this privilege that I was able to stick it out long enough to find a niche. There are talented academics who can't get a toehold in the academy, no matter how hard they try.

Fast forward through a whole PhD. (The years 2006 to 2009 were a blur and I don't remember anything that happened in 2008.) The six-week casual job had morphed into a sort-of, kind-of job and everyone now called me 'Doctor'. It was nice, but I didn't know what I should do next. I needed Mark's advice.

After another 20 minutes of explaining myself, he was starting to get it.

'So … you help PhD students get their PhD?'

'That sounds too simple,' I said, 'but yes. I suppose that's essentially what I do.'

'Simple is good', said Mark, smiling. 'Why is doing that important?'

'I'm not exactly sure what you mean. Why is what important?' I was starting to get a headache.

My sister smiled sympathetically across the table and poured me another glass of wine.

'Why is research education important?' Mark asked. He settled back in his chair. 'I know you love your job. Clearly you're good at it. You tell me RMIT has created all sorts of reasons to keep you around. What is it about this job that makes it special?'

I drank the wine my sister had poured. I was starting to feel a bit drunk, but it helped with the headache.

'I think it's the students ... but not because I feel sorry for them', I replied slowly. 'They're interesting. Their problems are very interesting. It's not really a teaching job because they're so smart.'

I went on to explain that most PhD students are over the age of 30 and that the age range was huge – some of them are in their seventies. People like me don't need to do teaching in a conventional sense. PhD students mostly need someone who will walk beside them and help them understand what they're going through. It's rewarding to see them finish. I guess I see them as the academic underdogs. Most people don't realise what a PhD is, and what it involves. The rare book or movie featuring a PhD student paints them as weird and nerdy.

I told Mark that this stereotype drives me crazy. In my opinion, PhD students are incredibly smart people doing work that could save the world.

Mark nodded. 'OK, that's your career mission statement.'

'What do you mean?' I asked, wondering if this was some kind of weird New Age American thing.

'A job is what you do for other people. A career is who you are', Mark said. He told me that a career mission is driven by a desire to solve a particular set of problems. Your job is just whoever happens to be paying for you to do your mission at any one time. A career potentially spans many of these mission-oriented jobs.

Thinking about myself as a custodian of a career, not an employee, was helpful and seemed like the perfect attitude in dealing with the bad boyfriend university. Mark explained that having a mission helps you decide how to work: which projects to say yes to and which ones to pass on. It helps you to decide whether to take a job or not. Mark then handed me a pen, pushed a napkin across the table and told me to write down my mission statement. After another glass of wine and some persuading I wrote the following:

> I think the world is in a bad state. PhD students
> are incredibly smart people who can help us solve

the most difficult problems. The problem is, so many of them are stuck in their PhD longer than they need to be. My mission is to help them to finish – by whatever means I can.

Doing a mission statement seemed ridiculous, but I'd drunk enough wine by this point and what I'd written looked pretty good to me. It was certainly a big problem, one I honestly believed could be the motivation for a life's work. If I thought about my work like this, in some small way I was helping to save the world – well, helping people who might be helping to save the world. Something inside me shifted. Suddenly I realised my knowledge was really a form of power, just like Michel Foucault said.

'So … what you're saying is that I'm not really a research fellow. I'm kind of an internal consultant? The person they have on hand to help solve problems with a particular group of students.'

Mark looked pleased. 'Exactly. If you become known just for your expertise, people will make the job you want for you.'

I laughed. 'Oh, Mark. You don't understand what universities are about, do you? They never make jobs for anyone.'

'You just finished telling me that they made jobs for the boys – jobs that you didn't get', Mark pointed out.

I shifted uncomfortably in my seat. 'That's not the same thing.'

'Isn't it?' Mark sipped his wine and looked at me with a raised eyebrow.

'So what do I do next?' I asked.

'Your next job will come via the internet', Mark said. 'People on the internet need to know about you and your mission.'

'So, um … I still don't know what to do.'

'Start a blog. You've got plenty to write about.'

———————

So I started a blog. I followed Mark's three simple rules of blogging:

1   People are on the internet looking for ways to solve their problems. Make useful content and readers will follow.

2   People will click away if you're not getting to the point quickly. Keep it short and stick to plain English.

3   Send a signal to your audience that you are professional and they can rely on you. The best way to do this is to post at the same time each week.

The rules work. Really, there's not much more to my success than that.

By 2012 the blog was a massive hit, but more to the point, I loved writing it, so it never felt like a chore. Life at work goes on as normal while I experience a strange, mostly secret celebrity. Then the phone rings while I'm at work. It's the Deputy Vice-Chancellor Research from the Australian National University. She just wants to talk. Would I come to Canberra for lunch?

Like Mark years before, my potential new employers didn't understand me. My resume was interesting, they said, and I was clearly very creative, but they wanted to know why I had worked at so many places. I realised that my resume made me look, well, feckless, especially to people who have had a standard old-skool academic career progression and had never worked on 'the outside'. I think they were a bit scared of hiring me because I didn't look like them. I didn't look like them because I wasn't like them.

There is no such thing as standard academic career progression anymore. What looked like creativity and innovation to them was just survival for me. In a rare moment of brilliance I told them I wasn't fickle, I was just the 'new normal academic'. I was the creature that the contemporary academy had made and I wasn't going to own the label of 'fickle' it forced on me. Not for a moment. And I was deadly serious about my work – I had a mission.

————

Higher education, in case you have been living under a rock and haven't noticed, is in a parlous state in many countries. Governments around the world spend less on, and expect more from, academics every year. There are now serious challenges to the university business model from free online content. If academics ever did live the life of the mind, it is difficult, if not impossible, to do so today.

Working in academia is not a certain life. You might have a stable job for now, but there's no reason to think that you might not one day find yourself marginalised, like I have been. It shouldn't be like this. You shouldn't have to have privilege, white or otherwise, to succeed. It should be about who can do the job, who's the smartest and who can teach well, but it's not.

You might be a new normal academic too. This book is offered as an aid to that life. It contains a set of tactics, resistance strategies and ideas for those experiencing a marginal academic existence – or those who wish to better understand what the new normal looks like.

2

BEING ACADEMIC?

As a woman, first in my family to go to university and pretender to the middle class, I don't feel like a 'natural' academic. I watch others around me perform social rituals such as the dreaded academic dinner party with an ease I never feel. I often apply theories I have learned from books on sociology and anthropology to help me make sense of what's going on around me. The posts in this chapter are really my own inner monologue, cleaned up for public consumption.

Some touch on issues that make me angry. Academic Assholes and the Circle of Niceness was the first post I published after I moved from RMIT University to the Australian National University (ANU). It enjoyed short-lived viral fame and continues to bounce around the internet as people discover and share it. Partly it's the title, which rolls off the tongue like the title of a Harry Potter book. As a way of announcing my presence on campus it was an (unintentional) genius move. I wrote it long before I started, about people at RMIT, but my new colleagues thought it must be a declaration of war against the bullies in their midst. In my experience there are a lot fewer academic assholes at ANU than at other places I have worked, but it was a conversation starter with people in all kinds of positions, from PhD students to the Deans of Colleges. Everyone had a story to tell about an academic asshole they once knew.

I am the first in my family to attend university and get a doctorate – which might be the reason I have a deep-seated sense that I don't really belong here. This is not to say that people are unwelcoming or that I haven't carved out a space of sorts. Academia is slowly becoming a more diverse place, but most of my close academic friends are either first in family or non-white. Us 'outsiders' tend to stick together for comfort and protection. Many of us suffer from the imposter syndrome – a terrible fear that you are not good enough and will eventually be found out, or kicked out, despite being very successful on every objective measure. I reflect on this sense of 'unhomeliness' in The Academic Migrant Experience. The lack of diversity in academia is a topic I also tackled in People Like Us? I was surprised at the reaction to this post – or, should I say, the lack of reaction; it made barely a ripple on the internet. I don't think this means the post was not valid or well written – just that maybe people were uncomfortable thinking about academia as being anything less than a meritocracy.

Some of my posts have helped me process feelings more than others. In Memory of Flick was one of these. Flick was like my older sister and I miss her still. Editing that post made me cry a little. In our death-denying culture it can be difficult to recognise the effects of grief and sadness in academia. I tell Chung's story of losing his supervisor in The Big Chill, which is really a meditation on the different forms of academic love. The Valley of Shit is in the top ten most popular posts about academic emotions. It speaks of the lack of perspective you can come to have about your PhD and the progress you have made – and the feelings of inadequacy you can have as a result. This is the only post people consistently tell me they have printed out and put on their wall. What seems to resonate is my observation that well-meaning support from friends and family can feel more like pressure than help.

One of my personal favourites in this collection is What Not to Wear (the Academic Collection). This is a perfect example of the thought experiments I like to do, applying sociological theories to my everyday, practical academic problems. I still haven't nailed what to wear as an academic, but I have enjoyed compiling the Pinterest boards that this post inspired. May this group of posts at least help you get dressed for your next conference presentation!

ACADEMIC ASSHOLES AND THE CIRCLE OF NICENESS

Two of my favourite people in the academic world are Rachael Pitt (aka @thefellowette) and Nigel Palmer (@nontweetingNP). It's rare for all of us to be in one place at the same time, but whenever it happens we have a fine old time talking shop. Some time ago Rachael started calling us 'the B-Team' because we were all appointed at level B in the Australian university pay-scale system (academic Level B is not quite shitkicker, entry level academia – that's level A, just in case you were wondering – but it's pretty close). I always go home feeling a warm glow of collegiality after a B-Team talk. These meet-ups make me feel like being an academic is the best job in the entire world. Rachael reckons that this positive glow is a result of the 'circle of niceness' we create just by being together and talking about ideas with honesty and openness.

Just after I announced my appointment as Director of Research Training at ANU, the B-Team met to drink beer, eat chips and get our nerd on. We talked about many things: my new job, the ageing academic work-force, research student retention rates and so on. Then we got to gossiping – as you do. All of us had a story or two to tell about academic colleagues who had been rude, dismissive, passive-aggressive or even outright hostile to us in the workplace. We'd encountered this behaviour from people at levels C, D and E, further up in the academic pecking order, but agreed it was most depressing when our fellow level Bs acted like jerks.

As we talked, we started to wonder: do you get further in academia if you are a jerk?

Jerks step on, belittle or otherwise sabotage their academic colleagues. The most common methods are criticising their opinions in public (at a conference or in a seminar) or trash-talking them in private. Some ambitious sorts actively cut off others from opportunity, presumably because they see everyone else as the competition. I'm sure it's not just academics on the payroll who have to deal with jerky academic behaviour. I get many emails from PhD students who have found themselves on the receiving end – especially during seminar presentations.

I assume people act like jerks because they think they have something to gain – and maybe they are right. In his best-selling book *The No Asshole Rule*, Robert Sutton, a professor at Stanford University, has a lot to say on the topic of assholes in the workplace. The book is erudite and amusing in equal measure; well worth reading, especially for the final chapter, where Sutton examines the advantages of being an asshole. He cites work by Teresa Amabile, who did a series of controlled experiments using fictitious book reviews. While the reviews themselves essentially made the same observations about the books, the tone in which the reviewers expressed their observations was tweaked to be either nice or nasty. Amabile found nasty reviewers were perceived as more intelligent, competent and expert than nice ones.

Huh.

This reminded me of the nasty cleverness that some academics display when they comment on PhD students' work in front of their peers. Performing 'clever' is a way academics show off their scholarly prowess to each other, sometimes at the expense of the student. Cleverness is a form of currency in academia – 'cultural capital', if you like. If other academics think you are clever they will listen to you more. Being clever gets you invited to speak at other institutions, to sit on panels and join important committees and boards. In short, the appearance of cleverness is a route to power and promotion. If acting like an asshole in a public forum creates the perverse impression that you are more clever than others who do not, there is a clear incentive to behave this way.

Sutton claims only a small percentage of people who act like assholes are actually sociopaths (he amusingly calls them 'flaming assholes'). What is more concerning is Sutton's theory that asshole behaviour is contagious. It's easy for asshole behaviour to become normalised in the workplace because, most of the time, the assholes are not called to account. So it's possible that many academics are acting like assholes without even being aware of it.

How does it happen? The budding asshole has learned, perhaps subconsciously, that other people interrupt them less if they use stronger language. Being an asshole gets attention: more airtime in panel discussions and at conferences. Junior colleagues watch strong language being used and then imitate the behaviour, believing it to be the norm. No one publicly objects to the language being used, even if the student is clearly upset, and nasty behaviour is quietly reinforced. As time goes on, the department culture progressively becomes more poisonous. Students who are upset by the behaviour of academic assholes in positions of power are told 'This is how things are done around here'. Those who resist the asshole culture eventually end up feeling abnormal because, in a literal sense, they are (if being normal is behaving like an asshole). It's hard to stay somewhere when you feel marginalised, so the nice academics just drift away.

Not all academic cultures are infected by assholes, but many show signs of colonisation. This explanation makes some of the sicker academic cultures I've experienced make sense. It might explain why senior academics are sometimes nicer and more generous to their colleagues than those lower in the pecking order. If asshole behaviour is a route to power, those who already have positions of power in the hierarchy and are widely acknowledged to be clever have less reason to use it.

To be honest with you, seen through this lens my career trajectory makes more sense too. I am not comfortable being an asshole, although I'm not going to claim I've never been one. I've certainly acted like a jerk in public a time or two in the past, especially when I was an architecture academic, where a culture of vicious critique is totally normalised. But I'd rather collaborate than compete and I don't like confrontation. I have quality research publications and a good public profile for my scholarly work, yet I found it hard to get advancement in my previous institution. Now I wonder if this is because I am too nice and, as a consequence, people tended to underestimate my intelligence. I think it's no coincidence that my career has only taken off since I started the blog. The blog is a safe space for me to display my knowledge and expertise without having to get into a pissing match.

Like Sutton, I am deeply uncomfortable with the observation that being an asshole can be advantageous for your career. Sutton takes a whole book to talk through the benefits of not being an asshole and I want to believe him. He clearly shows that there are real costs to organisations for putting up with asshole behaviour.

Put simply, the people who are nice and clever leave. I suspect this happens in academia all the time. It's a vicious cycle that means people who are more comfortable being an asshole easily outnumber those who find this behaviour obnoxious.

Ultimately we are all diminished when clever people walk away from academia. So what can we do? It's tempting to point the finger at senior academics for creating a poor workplace culture, but I've experienced this behaviour from people at all levels of the academic hierarchy. We need to work together to break the circle of nastiness. Everyone should be aware of the potential bias to think nasty means clever. Clever comes in both nice and nasty packages. I think we would all prefer, for the sake of a better workplace, that people tried to be nice rather than nasty. This doesn't mean we need be less critical of each other's work. Criticism can be gently and firmly applied; it doesn't have to be laced with vitriol. It's hard to do, but wherever possible we should work on creating circles of niceness. We can do this by being attentive to our own actions. Next time you have to talk in public about someone else's work, really listen to yourself. Are you picking up a hint of asshole?

💬 ACADEMIC ARROGANCE

At the start of my academic career I taught 3-D computer modelling and animation to architecture students. When you have been teaching something for a while, especially if it's a technically difficult skill, you see people make the same newbie mistakes, over and over again. It's dangerously easy to forget that it's new people making these same mistakes and get, well, grumpy.

It's a short step from grumpy to arrogant. A student taught me this important lesson one day in a computer lab. I don't even remember what I was trying to teach her, but I do remember she was an infuriatingly slow learner. My impatience grew till eventually (and I'm ashamed to admit this) I literally grabbed the keyboard out of her hands and said something like 'No, no, no! You do it THIS way!'

To this student's credit she didn't let me get away with this poor teacherly behaviour. She gave me a public dressing down in front of 20 of her classmates. She told me what a crap teacher I was and exactly why I was doing a shitty job. Then she left.

All the other students just sat there, staring at me. I was both mortified and ashamed, but I had at least an hour of the class left, so I was forced to carry on. Somehow we made it through the lesson. As I was packing up my books at the end of the class, questioning whether I ever wanted to walk into another one in my life, one of the other female students approached me. She told me I had a lot of knowledge of the topic and she liked me personally, but that the other student had a point. At times I was coming across as arrogant and dismissive. She told me the other students were too scared to tell me that I was being an academic asshole and they complained to her instead.

The philosopher Michel Foucault pointed out that knowledge and power are so intimately related that we cannot really think about them separately. That day I learned the truth of this the hard way. Arrogance is the Dark Side of knowledge. Your position as teacher gives you more power than your students. No matter how old these students are, your behaviour can make them scared of you. I haven't always succeeded in being tolerant and gracious in the classroom since that day, but I always try my best.

I tell you this story because of a comment on a blog post that reminded me of the dangers of academic arrogance. 'A Little Bit Rattled' told me about her recent experience of presenting work in progress at a department seminar. After giving a half-hour talk, Rattled stopped for questions and was floored by the first comment, which suggested that she was wrong in 'a very aggressive and threatening' tone. Rattled then described a scene I have witnessed over and over again as an academic:

> this senior academic went on to berate me (in front of around twenty colleagues) for about ten minutes on these ideas which I had explicitly stated were preliminary ... this was extremely confronting and, even worse, completely off topic and un-constructive. I wasn't the only one who felt it was out of hand. Afterwards, a few academics (including my supervisor) and fellow students commented privately that how this person had spoken to me was completely appalling. Some audience members even said that just having witnessed it left them deflated and feeling anxious for the rest of the day.

Rattled said she understood that part of being an academic is learning to defend your ideas within a culture of vigorous critique. But what is the line, Rattled wondered, between the student/supervisor hierarchy and 'plain old bullying'? She asked if I had any advice for PhD students who might encounter similar problems.

First of all, Rattled, congratulations on picking yourself up and brushing yourself off. I'm happy to hear you rationalising this experience and moving on. Is this bullying? It's a difficult question to answer. It's probably helpful to think about why this happened in the first place, rather than giving it a label. What we have here, really, is a story of power.

Foucault, depressing old philosopher that he was, made some useful observations about the nature of power. (All those Foucault scholars out there are just going to have to bear with me here, OK? I'm keeping this simple.) Power is generative: it can make things happen, both good and bad. While it is impossible to escape from power relations (such as student/teacher), there is always the possibility of resistance. Therefore your problem, Rattled – and the problem of all new PhD students – is learning how to deal with the effects of power and how, and when, to resist.

Resistance is more effective if you understand exactly the kind of power problem you have on your hands. It's not always easy to tell, but here are two suggestions.

It's possible this academic – as I did in the instance of arrogance described earlier – saw in your presentation some common mistakes and misconceptions. Instead of remembering that you are a new person making an old mistake, the academic just let loose with their own pent-up frustration. This academic had the power to speak. The setting of the department seminar and their seniority gave them the power to hold the floor, drowning out your voice and (unfortunately) the voice of your supervisor.

There are some, but not many, ways to resist in this situation. Asking questions is the most effective tactic I have learned. Good questions are 'Can you give me an example of that?' or 'Can you tell me about a way you've solved this problem before?'. This is a gentle way to remind the speaker that you are a learner and to use their knowledge/power for good instead of evil.

The second possibility is that your ideas or your intelligence were threatening to this academic and he or she was seeking to take you down. In this case, the academic is enacting what philosopher Pierre Bourdieu would call 'symbolic violence' on you. I like to think about this as the academic version of the Māori *haka*: a war dance or threatening display that is designed to make you afraid.

Marian Petre and Gordon Rugg in their excellent book *The Unwritten Rules of PhD Research* compare academics to sharks who are attracted to 'blood in the water'. The purpose of symbolic violence is to get you to bleed – to show weakness and uncertainty. In poisonous academic cultures (like my own home discipline of architecture) your blood in the water may give others in the audience permission to start attacking you too. Once a whole lot of academics decide to pile on, it can get ugly pretty quickly. We've all attended an academic presentation like this at one time or another. It's never an edifying spectacle and says much more about the departmental culture than it does about the student's competence.

The best and perhaps only way to resist in this situation is to deny the aggressor blood. Try to stay as calm as possible. Fix your gaze straight on the speaker and let them finish then wait for a moment before you answer. Silence is a potent weapon. Pause long enough for everyone to feel uncomfortable and show other academics who might be tempted to have a go that you are not to be trifled with. Then reply as calmly and dismissively as possible: 'Thank you for your feedback, I'll think about that. Are there any other questions?'.

Here's my personal view: whatever the motivation, the behaviour, although probably quite normalised in many places, is just not good teaching. I don't care if people defend such behaviour on the basis that it 'toughens people up'. That's what they said about the cane in primary schools and we have got along fine without that for some time now. All of us have seen colleagues make this mistake. I think all of us have the responsibility to quietly take them aside after such an incident and let them know it's Just Not Cool.

THE ACADEMIC MIGRANT EXPERIENCE

At a dinner not so long ago I got into an interesting conversation with a third-generation academic who was complaining about her father giving her unsolicited advice on how to do her PhD. I joked that this was bound to be Thesis Whisperer Jnr's fate, but I couldn't help contrasting her stories with my own experience. My father was sincerely impressed when I started my PhD and pleased as punch when I completed it, but he would never have dreamed of giving me advice on how to do it. You see, I'm a first-generation academic. An academic migrant, if you like.

My parents were intelligent, but largely self-educated. My father graduated with a trade certificate in industrial chemistry, very short of a university degree. My mother only just made it into high school and left when she was just fourteen. Due to the far-sighted educational policies of the Whitlam government in the early 1970s, my sister and I were the first members of our family able to go to university. University opened my eyes to another world – one that seemed defined by wealth and privilege. Out of a class of around 60, there were only three of us who had not gone to a fee-paying private school. My parents cared about my education, but they couldn't afford to pay for it. I went to whatever school was nearest my house. My education wasn't terrible, but wearing glasses and being interested in learning meant I was an instant target for bullying. Classrooms were often disrupted by kids who were bored as hell and being forced to have an education against their will.

The differences between the private school kid world and mine sound subtle now, but trust me when I say their effects were profound. I worked in a local takeaway shop; they worked in upscale department stores and bookstores. I went to goth clubs and drank gin; they went to wine bars and listened to jazz. I read trashy science fiction and romance novels; they read the latest Booker prize novels and, you know, classics, probably from their parents' bookshelves. We had no bookshelves because my father did not believe in spending money on books – he believed in the library. I lived in the suburbs and did not own a car; they lived in older-style, lovingly renovated period homes and drove themselves around in cute little hatchbacks gifted to them on their 18th birthday.

My new private school friends welcomed me into their world without judgment and I'm grateful. You see, those private school kids taught me how to be middle class. These middle-class ways often boiled down to quite simple things. For instance, I had never eaten pesto or drunk plunger coffee until my first year of uni –

in fact, I didn't even know what pesto was, or that coffee could come any other way but powdered and in a tin.

Luckily my parents had worked tirelessly on my speech at home, correcting me whenever I spoke like a 'bogan';* I suspect it would have been much more difficult to fit in otherwise. To this day, people at universities in Melbourne express shock when they hear where I grew up and went to school, such is the extent to which I learned to be like Them. It's not a coincidence that the majority of my friends at work are first-generation academics too. Migrants often feel an affinity for each other.

You are probably wondering why I am telling you my migrant story. Well, since having that conversation with a third-generation academic, I have been wondering how our upbringing might affect our experience of academia. Studies of experiences of 'first-timers' in undergraduate courses show that having university-educated parents is a decided advantage. Studies of first-generation academics' PhD experiences are in their infancy.

Is it harder to be a PhD student when you are an academic migrant as well? When I started my under-

---

*   Wikipedia defines 'bogan' as 'a derogatory Australian and New Zealand slang word used to describe a person whose speech, clothing, attitude and behaviour exemplify values and behaviour considered unrefined or unsophisticated'. That's pretty much it, but it also suggests a love of muscle cars and AC/DC.

graduate degree I didn't have many study skills; they weren't taught at school and my parents didn't know how to help me at home. I didn't even know how to take useful reading notes until halfway through my PhD. I've had to learn things about writing that I should have known long before I got to university. Things like the role of topic sentences; the difference between 'then' and 'than', 'that' and 'which'; the proper use of 'also'; and how verbs work to boost argumentative 'voice'. Was it that I just wasn't paying attention in class all those years?

Perhaps.

I've often thought of my migrant status as a handicap, but now I wonder if that's really the case. Maybe there are some advantages to learning how to be an academic from scratch? Many of us probably deal with the pressure of parental expectation, but I imagine a parent with actual PhD experience could be quite annoying. I suspect I would not have appreciated my father telling me how to write my introduction.

Of course, being a 'normal' academic is not just a case of being able to write properly. Over the last couple of years I've been studying the role of food in academia on social media through a hashtag project called #refreshmentswillbeprovided. Basically, every time I see food in academic settings I take a picture and record the circumstances. By using the hashtag, many others around the world have joined in, sharing their own academic culinary experiences. Observing all this food has made me realise just how much academic business is conducted at dinner tables. You need a little-recognised (but highly valuable) skill set to deal with this aspect of academic life.

I know what pesto is now and I buy my coffee as beans, not in a tin. I don't embarrass myself by not recognising a foodstuff at dinner anymore. But I had to learn how to cope with the academic dinner party – and it took a long time to feel comfortable at one. If I'm entirely honest, I still find them difficult sometimes. Big questions of class and privilege are opened up through simply looking at food. Are you disadvantaged, career-wise, if you can't hold your own in the sometimes excruciatingly polite conversations that take place at the academic dinner table? I'm not sure, but Thesis Whisperer Jnr certainly knows what fork to use. I'm looking forward to giving him unsolicited advice about his PhD when – and if – the time comes. Do you have hard-earned middle-class privilege? Pay it forward.

▪▪▪ PEOPLE LIKE US?

Some 15 years ago I used to regularly meet up with my friend and fellow computer nerd Joe in the university cafe for lunch. We were both working casually at multiple universities and hating the financially strapped, perilous lifestyle that came with it. We have both moved on and now live in different states, but back then those lunches were good therapy for both of us. There is nothing quite as satisfying as bitching to someone who truly understands how crap your work situation is.

One lunch in particular stands out for me. At the time we'd both decided enough was enough with the casual work and were looking for more permanent work in academia. It has to be said that neither of us was having much luck. I barely waited to put in my lunch order before debriefing Joe on my latest unsuccessful job interview. Once again, I had been passed over for a man who, I felt, was less qualified than me. This time the department in question had even offered to pay me double to make sure I saw out the semester because this 'replacement' couldn't actually teach the subjects he'd been hired for. Years later I learned through back channels that the Dean of the faculty had passed on me because two women in the department were fighting and he didn't want to 'add more fuel to the fire'.

I wish I'd known this crap was going on in the background because it was my fifth knock-back and I was beginning to seriously question my sanity. At the time I didn't understand that people don't get jobs in academia just because they are good at stuff like teaching. Connections, histories, reputations, gender, class – they all matter. At the time I bought into the myth of the meritocracy. I honestly thought that being good at your job and making sure students enjoyed and valued your teaching was enough. Now it's perfectly obvious why a professor who had run out of soft money would make sure his best research assistant got hired into a permanent role.

So I got my feminist rant on to Joe, who ate his lunch and patiently listened to me for around 20 minutes, until I had exhausted my rage. Then he said something I have never forgotten: 'Inger. I understand you being pissed off. But consider this. There are some women on permanent staff in that architecture department. There are no Asians.'

I stopped mid-chew.

Joe is of Asian descent. Actually, I'm not even sure of his precise ethnic background – I've never asked. He was just 'Joe' to me. This is not to say that I don't 'see colour'; I'd be lying if I said I never noticed. It's just that Joe and I were similar in so many ways. I had never thought consciously about the implications of Joe having an Asian background and me having some kind of mongrel British one. Or, more precisely, if I did think about it I had dismissed it as irrelevant.

But suddenly I realised race did matter – at least, it seemed, in academic hiring practices. There were plenty of talented people of Asian descent, like Joe, who studied architecture with me. Plenty of these people taught architecture in that department sessionally, just like I did. But at the time there was not one person of Asian descent on permanent staff, while about 20 per cent of them were women. If the past was anything to go by, I had much more chance of getting a job in that department than Joe did, and that was clearly wrong. He was better at computer graphics teaching than I was and had not even been shortlisted for the job I had just missed out on.

What really tore me up, though, was the way Joe talked about it. So calmly and so matter-of-factly. Clearly he had noticed such inequities all his life and this was but one more instance. I asked him if he ever got angry and he answered 'Yes, of course!'. But he pointed out that getting angry all the time is exhausting. I nodded – I had come to the same conclusion about sexism. So we tacitly agreed to change the subject and talked about computers for the rest of lunch. I went home afterwards feeling deeply troubled.

I still feel troubled whenever I think of this moment.

The fact that race didn't figure in my thoughts about academic hiring practice was, I realised, a symptom of my own white privilege. I had assumed that being a woman mattered far more than being Asian when it came to discrimination in hiring decisions. But the numbers don't lie. In fact, I just checked on the website for that particular department. There are still no Asian Australians on permanent staff. There is now one person with a Greek name and another who is Italian – I suppose that's progress? I don't have the figures on racial diversity in academia on hand, but this one architecture department certainly doesn't reflect the diversity of students it enrols.

How does this happen? Well, just like the cancerous growth of academic assholes through a department, racism persists through the small actions of everyone, every day. A good example is my friend Peter, who is widely published and a great teacher. Privately educated and the son of a surgeon, Peter has the kind of middle-class gloss I can only dream of possessing. Erudite, charming and funny, Peter performs at those academic dinner parties, the ones that I despise, with aplomb. But Peter is also of Asian descent and despite many attempts, did not get hired onto permanent staff in the department where Joe and I used to work either. Eventually he moved interstate and got an excellent job, tellingly in a department where the Dean was also of Asian descent.

Coincidence? I don't think so. For years I watched Peter suffer persistent, silent racism in academia. He told me about an unsuccessful phone interview he did just before he landed his first permanent academic job. Apparently he was on 'the long shortlist' for an academic job and the hiring committee wanted to see if they should move him to the 'short shortlist'. I asked him why there was an interview for that and he replied – again, totally matter-of-factly and with a touch of wry humour – 'Oh, they saw my name and probably wanted to confirm that I could speak English'.

I had no words.

I encourage you to look around you for a moment. Is it just me, or is academia in Australia very white? What gives, people? Are academic hiring committees racist? Or just largely unconscious of the operation of white privilege? Do they just keep hiring 'people like us' without even noticing it's happening? Granted, some departments, notably in science, are a little more diverse, but the fact that we can point to them as different is telling, don't you think?

On any given day, inequities of all kinds are being earnestly and carefully discussed in the seminars, cafes and lunch rooms of academia. Articles about racism written by academics appear in newspapers all the time, but we rarely subject ourselves to the same level of scrutiny and critique. I'm far from the first person to say that privilege is often mistaken as being normal – as 'just how things are'. It can take effort to notice the systems that perpetuate privilege in action – and there can be pushback if you question the way things are. But for me, staying silent is no longer an option.

💬 IN MEMORY OF FLICK

In early 2013 one of my dearest friends had a fatal heart attack while sitting at her computer at home. She was only 54. Flick (whom I never once called by her actual name, Felicity Jones) was 12 years older than me. I never thought about it this way when she was alive, but now she's gone I realise she was like the big sister I never had. I miss Flick because she was an accomplished human being. I've reflected on what I learned from her over the years and I think some of these lessons apply to being an academic, so I'm going to tell you three of them.

Accept your failings, tell a story and laugh at them

Flick would have been the first one to say she was terrible with money and didn't like cleaning the house. When she died her paperwork was a mess and she left behind a truly amazing number of unpaid parking fines. Although she had drafted a will, it seemed she never got around to signing it. We all managed to have a laugh about this in the terrible week after she died because it was just so typical.

None of these omissions happened because she was stupid. Far from it – she'd gone back to school in the 1990s and earned a Masters by research. Flick just had trouble paying attention to details. Terrible trouble. She tried all kinds of things to fix her attention problems, most of which didn't work. Finally she was diagnosed with ADHD at age 50 and was relieved to finally have an explanation. The treatment didn't seem to help, though.

While most of us hide our failings from the world, Flick would tell funny stories about her stuff-ups, with great relish and a hearty belly laugh that invited you to laugh with her. Flick's acceptance of her own failures went along with acceptance of other people's failings. She was the person that everyone confided in because she honestly didn't judge. You could tell her terrible things about your inner thoughts and she would listen carefully and sympathetically. She only dispensed wisdom if she really thought it would help – she never, ever gave unsolicited advice.

So much time in academia is dedicated to the pursuit of perfection, it can be easy to forget that stories of failure are often more interesting – and human. The late great Carrie Fisher observed that sharing her vulnerabilities and mental illness created a community of support around her. I've found the same thing happens on *The Thesis Whisperer*. Academics are so accustomed to being the expert in the room that it's hard to admit when we are wrong. We don't talk much about things like horrible peer reviews or failed grant attempts. We are encouraged to be 'resilient', which is fine, but sometimes this resilience narrative becomes a shield, a way of denying there are any hurt feelings. I'm pleased that stories of my own failure have resonated so much with others. While working to accept your failings you may find solutions – or not.

Laughter helps regardless.

There are only actions and consequences

Flick was a great parent because she approached the task with intelligence, care and diligence. Her adult daughters genuinely enjoyed spending time with her – a testament to her success. I used to ask Flick for parenting advice because I aspire to be a parent/friend when Thesis Whisperer Jnr grows up. Flick often talked about how important it was to equip your kids for the world, but to never fall into the trap of feeling sorry for them. The key, she claimed, was to hold back from fixing all their problems. If you swoop in to save your kids all the time, she said, it sends the message that you don't have confidence in their ability to fix things for themselves. The job of a parent is to help build confidence, not undermine it.

In my view, many research supervisors could take a leaf from Flick's book of parenting. I often encounter supervisors who think their primary job is to edit their student's writing, but correcting is not helpful past a certain point because it disempowers people. It is far better to spend time teaching students how to avoid the mistakes in the first place. Standing back is not the same as being neglectful. Research students are highly capable adults. We need to respect their abilities and let them fix their own mistakes.

Be who you are

It was always easy to buy presents for Flick. Her taste was eclectic and she was enthusiastic about all kinds of stuff and would share that enthusiasm willingly. She liked steampunk, Celtic tattoos, spiky high-heeled boots, Led Zeppelin, Georgette Heyer novels, the history of Wales, Nat King Cole, quilting, cable knitting, corsets, computer games, Jamie Oliver, purple hand luggage, Vince Jones, LittleBigPlanet and cupcakes – I could go on and on.

The thing I will remember most about Flick and her interests will be her enjoyment of them. No matter what anyone else thought, she was confident that what she liked was interesting and worthwhile. This was an attractive quality that drew people to her. For instance, I'll admit that I never understood her fascination with the online community Second Life. I'll admit I was judgmental and thought Second Life was a waste of time, but I kept my thoughts to myself because Flick threw herself into it with enthusiasm and built relationships with many people there. After she died it was some measure of comfort for me to read about the grief within this online community. Second Life was a creative outlet for Flick; a lot of the stuff she made in there was beautiful. The self she made in Second Life was the most pure expression of her aesthetic interests.

What I take from this observation, for research practice particularly, is the importance of curiosity and the joy of following your interests with enthusiasm. I like to write academic papers about odd things: whingeing, food, hobbies. Sometimes I have a hard time getting these papers into the peer review process, perhaps because these topics don't seem important to journal editors. I write papers on more banal topics just to 'get runs on the board'. While banal papers are much easier to publish, my heart is not in them and they take an agonisingly long time to complete. I guess Flick would say sometimes we have to stick with the things that interest us in the face of the indifference of others, gatekeepers or not. Eventually, if you persist, such writings will find an audience who will appreciate them.

Thank you, dear reader, for staying with me this far and indulging my need to pay homage to my friend. Writing this helped me process the loss just a little bit. Vale Flick. We'll always miss you.

💬 THE BIG CHILL

When Tolstoy said 'All happy families are alike; each unhappy family is unhappy in its own way' he could have been talking about research supervision. When it goes right, the research supervisor/student relationship is the best kind of teaching and learning experience there is. I'm going to meditate on how a relationship with your supervisor can bring you joy by telling you a sad story (hey, my boss doesn't call me the Mistress of Misery for nothing!).

This story is about a student I know, let's call him Chung because not all the fake names I use should be Anglo-Saxon in origin. Chung worked well with his supervisor; in fact, the two quickly became close. Both shared a passion for climate science and drinking craft beers. Chung was new to town and his supervisor regularly invited him around for dinner with his wife and kids. What really made the relationship work was mutual respect. While Chung's supervisor was clearly the leader of the science team, Chung didn't feel like a student because his supervisor treated him like a valued and respected junior colleague. In the research education literature this is called something like ideal student–supervisor alignment. In less pompous terms, the two had found a way to be friends, despite the fact that one of them was in charge.

For the first couple of years, Chung attacked the work with energy and enthusiasm. He is a friendly and outgoing kind of guy, who, by his own admission, perhaps spends a bit too much time partying. Luckily Chung is super smart and can still make good progress on his research while hungover! Despite this active social life, Chung was not really plugged into the lab culture around him. Secrecy is a bit of a thing in science, from what I understand, especially if the work is truly new. No one else was actively involved in Chung's research, or really knew what he and his supervisor were doing together. The potential of the research was exciting; they had already mapped out a plan for years of work together.

Then Chung's supervisor got brain cancer.

It was a bad cancer too. Chung told me they call

this particular tumour 'the widow-maker' because most people who get it die within 18 months. But for Chung's supervisor, it was quicker. While he was still relatively well, Chung's supervisor went into hospital for a procedure to ease the pain. Unfortunately he got septicaemia and was sent to intensive care. Chung was only able to see his supervisor once in the hospital. The visit upset him; the person in the bed was not the person he knew. Chung's supervisor eventually recovered from the infection, but he was so weakened that all the doctors could do was make him comfortable and send him home to die.

Chung tried to carry on the work alone, but the image of his dying supervisor haunted him. It was the beginning of a dark time. The work Chung was doing was so bound up with his supervisor's life and personality that it was a constant reminder of the terrible suffering that Chung knew was happening. He found it harder and harder to focus and the project lost crucial momentum. The situation was not helped by our death-denying Western culture. All the academics in the department were sympathetic and concerned about Chung's welfare, but no one offered to take him on, even temporarily, because that would mean accepting that Chung's supervisor was about to die. And he did, aged just 46.

While an email was circulated among the academic

staff, no one in management thought to break the news of Chung's supervisor's death to his student – can you even believe that? Chung found out about his friend's death through an email from an administrator asking him to clean out his supervisor's office. A truly terrible way to hear about losing someone close. The workplace had become a scene of trauma and Chung found going to work a struggle. He spent hours at his desk doing essentially nothing, while berating himself for not getting a move on. His candidature time was ticking on and the sense of urgency turned into a weird kind of disconnected panic. It was at this point that a friend, who had grown concerned about Chung's uncharacteristic behaviour, brought him to my office for a cup of tea.

We discussed what had happened and I suggested he visit the counselling centre. He followed my advice. Later he told me that it was only in the counsellor's office that he was able to cry for the first time. He cried for a whole hour while the counsellor sat with him and handed over tissues. On a second visit the counsellor helped him come up with a plan to extend his candidature and ease the anxiety. In the end, Chung had himself diagnosed with depression in order to be eligible for an extension to compensate for lost time. It's important to note that Chung was not really depressed. He was just deeply sad and grieving for his friend, which is completely normal. It is a bizarre quirk of our system that a problem like this has to be medicalised. Ironically, shortly after being granted his medical leave, Chung broke his right elbow and was unable to take more medical leave because he had run out.

I'm happy to report that, slowly, things began to get better for Chung.

He was given a new panel of supervisors, which was positive, but not without its challenges. No one else really understood the work that had been done. Chung's new supervisors made suggestions which seemed to be tangents. He felt a sense of loyalty to his dead supervisor and initially resisted the changes, but he quickly realised this was not a productive way to behave. His friend would want him to finish his PhD, first and foremost. The changes ended up being a good thing and led the research in another exciting direction.

Chung told me he only really discovered how truly amazing his supervisor was after he climbed out of his grief cave and started working properly again. While there is an amazing range of expertise at ANU, Chung needed to draw on his dead supervisor's international network for help to finish his PhD. Chung found out that people all over the world mourned his supervisor's death. Academics from Japan, London, the Netherlands and France contributed advice, equipment, samples and data. I guess this is the academic equivalent of bringing around a stew and putting it in the fridge of the bereaved; a tangible form of respect for the dead and help for those who live on. It was weird seeing obituaries written that said nothing about their work together, but Chung was touched by the obvious sense of loss in the community.

Chung told me he felt a bit like an adopted child of his supervisor's extended academic family – an orphan now, who needed help and nurturing. My friend Tseen Khoo says that 'networking' is often presented to research students in extremely simplistic ways and this story is a good demonstration of her point. Academic networks are surprisingly robust things that are held together, I believe, by a strange form of love. Love for each other? Well, platonic love of course (most of the time!). Love for the work? Definitely. This is what my friend Rachael Pitt calls 'the circle of niceness' and we can really see it in operation in this story.

Chung did other positive things. He kept in touch with his old supervisor's actual family and still helps foster his supervisor's young children's interest in science. He said he knew he was getting better when he participated in a fundraising walk against cancer and met a lot of people who were still in the grief cave. It was only then he realised he'd moved beyond sad into a better place. He still felt the loss of his friend like a missing tooth; but the pain had lessened and in its place was a gap he would just have to learn to live with.

Chung connected strongly with his broader research community, becoming deeply involved in our Thesis Boot Camp program, helping others move past difficulties with writing. Now that he has graduated we miss him dearly.

This is a sad story, but it's also, in a strange way, a lovely one. It speaks of the genuine attachment that academic work can produce between supervisors and their students. Only a few students (I hope) would have had this experience, or will experience it in the future. If this is you, rest assured it can get better. Seek help from your university. The systems aren't perfect, but if Chung's experience is anything to go by, there are people who will go out of their way to help you. I would hope your academic family will be there for you.

 THE VALLEY OF SHIT

I have a friend doing his PhD at the moment – let's call him Dave.

I admire Dave. He is a full-time academic with a young family and must treat his PhD as just one job among many. But rather than moan about not having enough time, Dave looks for creative time-management solutions. Despite the numerous demands on him, Dave is a generous colleague. He willingly listens to my work problems over coffee and always has an interesting suggestion or two. His resolute cheerfulness and 'can do' attitude is an antidote to the culture of complaint which seems, at times, to pervade academia.

I was therefore surprised when, for no apparent reason, Dave started talking negatively about his PhD and his ability to finish on time. All of a sudden he seemed to lose confidence in himself, his topic and the quality of the work he had done. Dave is not the only person who seems to be experiencing these feelings lately. I have another friend, let's call him Andrew, doing his PhD at a prestigious university. Like Dave, Andrew approaches his PhD as a job, applying the many time-management skills he had learned in his previous career as a software engineer. His research is groundbreaking and Andrew has turned out an impressive number of papers, much to the delight of his supervisors. So I was deeply shocked when Andrew emailed me to say he was going to quit. He claimed everything he did was no good and it took a number of intense phone calls to convince him to carry on.

Both these students were trapped in a phase of PhD study I have started to call 'the Valley of Shit'.

The Valley of Shit is that period of your PhD, however brief, when you lose perspective, confidence and belief in yourself. There are a few signs you are entering the Valley of Shit. You can start to think your whole project is misconceived, or that you do not have the ability to do it justice. Or you might seriously question if what you have done is good enough and start feeling like everything you have discovered is obvious, boring and unimportant. As you walk deeper into the Valley of Shit it becomes more and more difficult to work and you start seriously entertaining thoughts of quitting.

I call this state of mind the Valley of Shit because you need to remember you are merely passing through it, not stuck there forever. Valleys lead to somewhere else – if you can but walk for long enough. Unfortunately, the Valley of Shit can feel endless because you are surrounded by towering walls of brown stuff which block your view of the beautiful landscape beyond.

The Valley of Shit is a terrible place to be because, well, not to put too fine a point on it, it smells. No one else can (or really wants to) be down there, walking with you, so you have the Valley of Shit all to yourself. This is why, no matter how many reassuring things people say, it can be hard to believe that the Valley of Shit actually ends. In fact, sometimes those reassuring words can only make the Valley of Shit more oppressive. The problem with being a PhD student is that you are likely to have been a star student all your life. Your family, friends and colleagues know this about you. Their confidence in you is real – and well founded. While rationally you know they are right, their optimism and soothing 'You can do it' mantras can start to feel like extra pressure rather than encouragement.

I have spent more than my fair share of time in the Valley of Shit. I was Thesis Whispering while I was doing my PhD – so you can imagine the pressure I felt to succeed. An inability to deliver a good thesis, on time, would be a sign of my professional incompetence on so many levels. The Valley of Shit would start to rise up around me whenever I starting second-guessing myself. The internal monologue went something like this: 'My supervisor, friends and family say I can do it – but how do they really know? What if I disappoint all these people who have such faith in me? What will they think of me then?'

Happily, all my fears were groundless. My friends, teachers and family were right: I did have it in me, but the smell of all those days walking in the Valley of Shit stays with you. So I don't want to offer you any empty words of comfort. The only advice I have is: just keep walking. By which I mean just keep writing, doing experiments, analysis or whatever, even if you don't believe there is any point to it. Remember that you are probably not the right person to judge the value of your project or your competence right now.

Try not to get angry at people who try to cheer you on – they are only trying to help. Although you are alone in the Valley of Shit, there is no need to be lonely. Find a fellow traveller or two and have a good whinge, if that helps. But beware of indulging in this kind of 'troubles talk' too much, lest you start to feel like a victim.

Maybe try to laugh at it just a little.

You may be one of the lucky ones who only experience the Valley of Shit once in your PhD, or you might be unlucky and find yourself there repeatedly, as I did. I can completely understand those people who give up before they reach the end of the Valley of Shit – but I think it's a pity. Eventually it has to end, because the university won't let you do your PhD forever. Even if you never do walk out the other side, one day you will just hand the thing in and hope for the best.

💬 THE MOUNTAIN OF HAPPY

Someone on Twitter, I forget precisely who, suggested I do a follow-up post to The Valley of Shit (which describes the state of mind where your thesis seems terrible and you lose confidence, and all perspective) and call it 'The Mountain of Happy'. I can never resist a good title, so I logged in to WordPress, created the post and dashed off a couple of lines: 'The mountain of happy is the opposite of the Valley of Shit' and 'Something about dizziness or altitude?' ... and then I sat there, staring at the screen. Realising I had nothing more to say, I saved the post and moved on to other things. A lot of other things. As a result, the seed for this post sat in the queue for many months.

In one sense this is business as usual for me. I usually have around 37 half-written posts sitting in the queue. Some are just placeholders for ideas and nothing more. Every now and then I go in and clean up the queue, but I could never quite bring myself to delete the Mountain of Happy post. Occasionally I would open it and stare at those two lines for ages before realising ... I still had nothing.

Then I started to worry.

Deleting the post seemed to be an admission that I had nothing nice to say about the PhD process – which just isn't true. I wouldn't spend my life helping PhD students if I thought it was all so terrible. But it worried me that I seemed unable to write a positive post about the PhD experience. Did it mean I really was the 'Mistress of Misery', as my boss sometimes called me?

The post started to feel like a sore tooth until I visited the Queensland University of Technology to give a keynote at the Creative Industries student conference. The talk is one I've given a couple of times that explores the emotional complexities of the PhD experience via my sad addiction to romance novels. During question time at the end, a student in the audience, Kirsty, made some interesting comments about struggle. I encouraged her to write a post about her thoughts, but thinking about the PhD as a struggle suddenly gave me a way into this post.

If I had to list the three moments of my life when I stood on top of the Mountain of Happy they would be, in this order:

1   Seeing Thesis Whisperer Jnr's face for the first time.
2   Marrying Mr Thesis Whisperer.
3   Walking across the stage to accept my PhD testamur from the Chancellor of the University of Melbourne.

Those three brief periods of delirious happiness only came after an extended period of struggle.

Pregnancy was not easy for me. I spent nine months struggling with the inaccurately named 'morning sickness'. Like all young couples, Mr Thesis Whisperer and I struggled initially to adjust to each other before we got married. And the PhD? Well, the PhD was the definition of struggle. I spent a lot of time in the Valley of Shit, but the day I got the degree, and stood at the top of the Mountain of Happy, all the angst magically dropped away.

In *The Seven Basic Plots: Why We Tell Stories*, Christopher Booker claims there are a limited number of plots in literature, all with different kinds of struggle. In a story, struggle can provide the backdrop against which happiness can be experienced more fully. Certainly academic work, particularly scientific discovery, is often framed as some kind of heroic story where the researcher struggles towards knowledge.

Consider the discovery of the role *Helicobacter pylori*, a simple stomach bacteria, plays in stomach ulcers (a topic close to my heart because I suffered through having one most of my PhD). The way this discovery is recounted in the media often echoes the plot types Booker talks about. Throughout the 20th century, German researchers tried in vain to get the scientific community interested in the idea that stomach complaints were not nervous complaints, but diseases with bacterial origins. Australian scientists Dr Barry Marshall and Dr Robin Warren did a series of experiments and testing regimes and discovered that a single strain of bacteria (*H. pylori*) was responsible. Dr Marshall (our hero) deliberately infects himself with the bacteria to demonstrate the efficacy of antibiotics. Fame, fortune and Nobel Prizes follow – your classic happy ending. There are numerous other examples of this type of mythologising in science. There is less of it in the humanities perhaps, but we certainly still find 'heroes': Foucault, Derrida and the like.

There is no inherent problem with mythologising, but I think we need to be careful of framing all academic work this way. Excessive struggle, to no purpose, is not good for anyone. Poor supervision can certainly lead to pointless struggle. But struggle itself can often be a good thing, productive of discovery and change. I guess that's why writing positive upbeat stories about the PhD and academia ultimately bores me. You can stand on top of the Mountain of Happy for a little while. Once you have admired the view and basked in your accomplishment there's really not much else to do up there. Eventually you must trudge back down into the Valley, where all the really interesting stuff happens.

WHAT NOT TO WEAR (THE ACADEMIC COLLECTION)

What exactly does one wear when giving a keynote lecture?

This question perplexed me during the whole of 2011 because I started to be invited as a guest speaker to various conferences and seminars. Keynote speakers are there to set the tone and respond to the theme of the event – but dressing for this gig is a sartorial challenge of no small order. In fact, deciding what to wear is not easy when you are an academic – even for men. We don't have the luxury of suit-as-uniform like our counterparts in the corporate world. We often have to front classrooms full of people barely out of puberty and then go to a committee meeting with peers and straight on to an academic dinner party.

When I was an architect, it was easy – I just had a closet full of black. Since I left the profession it's been difficult to find my own style and accommodate my increasingly middle-aged body. To make it easier, for some time now my twin sister Anitra and I have been creating our own academic clothing taxonomy to deal with this complexity (it's very handy to have a twin sister who is also an academic to help workshop these problems). The academic clothing taxonomy is basically a series of silly wardrobe nicknames, expanded beyond the classic Little Black Dress to encompass any number of occasions. Presently it includes the Definitive White Shirt, the Sexy Librarian Number, the Meet-the-People Dress, the Last-Minute Tutorial Saviour and the Perfect Pants – to name but a few.

Stay with me, now – there's a serious point coming up soon, I promise.

Each of these items of clothing must be in our wardrobes at all times because they correspond to certain social and academic workplace challenges. The Definitive White Shirt goes with anything, including jeans, and makes you look put-together with minimal effort. The Meet-the-People Dress is the sort of outfit which takes you from classroom to drinks before an evening lecture without looking like you are trying too hard (the Spring Show is the art/design exhibition version). The Last-Minute Tutorial Saviour (LMTS) was developed when Thesis Whisperer Jnr was under the age of three and I needed to pull off casual and classroom-ready ten minutes after getting out of bed. It was therefore crucial that the LMTS was good at hiding inevitable toddler 'yogurt hand' marks.

These Wardrobe Types are like Platonic Forms; Anitra and I are always on the hunt for new and more perfect manifestations of them. We have been known to ring each other excitedly when we find a fine example of a Type and, since we are basically the same shape and size, sometimes we buy two so the other won't miss out (it's a twin thing). The Sexy Librarian Number (SLN) is perhaps the most elusive. The SLN is the kind of dress you need when presenting a paper at a conference. It's a dress that makes you look 'academic' without being frumpy and, despite the 'sexy' label, it cannot be revealing. I started to think of the Keynote Dress (KND) as the older sister to the SLN. The KND needs to step it up a notch in the 'serious academic' stakes, but doesn't need to be as over the top as my one and only I'd-like-to-thank-the-academy Academic Awards Night Ensemble (a fiendishly difficult dressing challenge, let me tell you – similar to the Graduation Outfit, but unfortunately not covered by a robe).

Don't even get me started on the shoe problem, OK?

Going out shopping deliberately for a Wardrobe Type virtually guarantees that you will not find an example, especially if there's a deadline by which you need to acquire it. I was therefore relieved when I found my first Keynote Dress, unexpectedly, while casually browsing in a department store on my lunch break. I remarked on Twitter that I was relieved that this wardrobe challenge had been achieved and was surprised by the number of responses. Clearly many other academics could relate to, and were interested in, the numerous challenges of academic dressing. It seemed my sister and I are not alone in the nickname thing; @trishmorgan told me about her Lucky Conference Blouse (must add that to my list). I was interested when @alisonseaman told me that her creative dress sense was too creative for the other Fine Art academics and when @deborahbrian started to talk about the 'bloke fashion' trend in archeology, I realised this academic dressing thing deserved some serious attention.

Does what we wear have career implications? An article by Alison Schneider, sent to me by @fashademic, suggested it might:

There was just one problem with the English department's job candidate: his pants. They were polyester, green polyester, and the members of the hiring committee considered that a serious offence. For 10 minutes they ranted about the cut, the color, the cloth. Then and only then did they move on to weightier matters.

They say you should dress for the job you aspire to, not the one you have. So should you have to dress the part to get an academic job? If we are to believe Pierre Bourdieu, the French social theorist, the answer would be 'yes' because we all possess 'cultural capital'. With apologies for the gross simplification of an elegant social theory, cultural capital can be thought of as an asset, just like money, property, jewellery and other possessions. Cultural capital is basically knowing how to behave and act a part in a society through possessing certain 'props', like the 'right' outfit for a particular occasion. We accumulate cultural capital by immersion – by constant exposure to how others around us dress, behave and act and (mostly unconsciously) mimicking what we see.

An example of cultural capital at work is 'good taste'. Who decides what 'good taste' is? Well, everyone – and no one. Good taste is something that arises between us, which is why it's possible to have so many personal definitions at the same time. However, if Bourdieu is right, those personal definitions of good taste will start to converge when groups of people spend a lot of time living and working together. By this logic, every academic discipline will start to value different sorts of cultural capital – we can think of them as 'tribes' who share values and ways of doing things in common. PhD study is the perfect time to spend some time studying your academic tribe and acquiring your own store of academic cultural capital.

Acquiring academic cultural capital is much more than a matter of learning how to dress the part. Consider the problem of the literature review. Here you display your knowledge of what constitutes 'good' and 'bad' in a particular academic field. You do this by choosing and talking about the 'right' authors, in the 'right' way. Knowing what is 'right' is a form of cultural capital you have acquired through reading and talking with other academics. It is difficult to acquire this kind of academic cultural capital outside of the academy because you need models and feedback from others to learn how to perform it properly. Possessing and displaying the right cultural capital (in your writing, at least) is essential for building trust and credibility with your academic colleagues, so why not clothes too?

Writing this post made me feel a bit better about the amount of time I spent in 2011 agonising on the Keynote Dress – at least that's my excuse.

3

BEING PRODUCTIVE

Wherever I have worked in my life I have eventually developed a reputation as the 'technology expert'. I'm no expert, but I will admit to being an early adopter. I love gadgets and have a serious Apple habit, but unless you can program UNIX I don't think you can really claim to be a proper geek.

I had early exposure to digital technologies. My dad studied to be a dye house chemist in the 1960s, but became a computer programmer in the late '70s. His first computer job involved looking after mainframes, which took up whole rooms back then. I remember sitting under his desk making necklaces out of punched cards. Despite having computer geekery in my blood, I have never become a 'proper' computer nerd. Aside from a brief addiction to Zork in the '80s, I've never really enjoyed computer games and I don't have much aptitude for computer programming, much to my father's disappointment. I did marry a computer programmer, though, which cheered the old man up a bit.

It is not software proficiency which makes me 'geeky', but the attitude to using technology I developed in my childhood. I think this attitude is best summed up by the conversation I had with my father when he sat me down in front of our family's first PC. This was the early '80s and I had just turned twelve. As I recall, the encounter went something like this:

Dad: We're going to learn Basic. Type '10 PRINT "HELLO WORLD".'

Me: What if I hurt it?

Dad: What do you mean?

Me: What if I kill its brain?

Dad: You can't kill it. It's not alive. It doesn't have a brain.

Me: Then how does it, you know, do stuff?

Dad: The computer is stupid. It only does what you tell it to do. The only way you can hurt it is to type "format C colon".

(pause)

Dad: Please don't do that, by the way.

Me: OK. Can I play Zork now?

Early exposure gave me the confidence to face new technology without fear. I jump in and fiddle around, break some stuff and eventually figure things out, with the comforting knowledge that nothing I do (except typing 'format C colon') will cause lasting damage. I'm always on the hunt for a new piece of software or hardware to fix my academic productivity problems, which I talk about at length in this chapter.

Academic work is detail-focussed – I am not. In The Last 5 Per Cent Always Kicks My Ass, I talk about how 'finishing properly' and perfectionism are often conflated. This post struck a chord with many readers, who were sick of being accused of being perfectionistic when they were really trying to live up to the high expectations we put on academics for rigour and accuracy. As you'll have gathered by now, many posts I write come out of my personal experiences. My experience with EndNote at the end of my thesis was traumatic. EndNote vs … Everything Else is the story of a hunt for the perfect reference manager, which was also an opportunity to reflect on the complex set of factors that you need to take into account when organising technology to support academic work. In Shut Up and Write! I reflect on the spaces used for academic work and why noisy, even communal spaces can lead to startling levels of productivity. It was this early work on the effects of working in community that led me to help start up the academic 'Shut Up and Write!' movement with my friends Jonathan and Tseen from The Research Whisperer blog, and the ANU version of the University of Melbourne Thesis Boot Camp program. Both are examples of how reflections on the blog have turned into initiatives to assist people in learning how to do academic work.

A Visit from the Procrastination Fairy is a reader favourite, but as I edited I found I had a lot more to say on the topic, so I added in some thoughts on the so-called imposter syndrome. I followed this post with Where Do Good Ideas Come From? Here I put together three different posts to make the argument that creativity is a process, or a set of techniques, not an intrinsic characteristic you do or don't have. I end with two posts on parenting that reflect on the impossibility of 'work–life balance'.

Reflecting on this group of posts about the paradox of academic productivity, I have come to the conclusion that there are no perfect answers. I'm all for efficiency and delivering to our 'stakeholders' (in this case, the taxpayers), but using sticks like performance metrics to force academics to be productive is going to fail if we don't take feelings, cultures and practices into account. These posts try to reflect the complex interaction of all the factors that stop us from doing as much as we would like to and my own, admittedly partial, solutions.

THE LAST 5 PER CENT ALWAYS KICKS MY ASS

The last 5 per cent of any project is the really detailed work, which just bores the hell out of me. I am great at starting projects and getting the majority of the hard work done, but finishing – really finishing something properly – is not my forte. The last 5 per cent of a journal article involves checking reference lists, formatting, looking for spelling mistakes and so on. I find this kind of work tedious and frankly I'm bad at it. My lack of competence makes me irritated, so I avoid or delay the last 5 per cent as long as possible. This tendency really holds me back – for instance, the last 5 per cent of the work on this book took me nearly a whole year.

Avoiding the last 5 per cent causes lots of problems. The tendency to declare 'good enough' too quickly inevitably means I must go back and fix something, usually when I really don't have time for it. My 95-percenter tendency is one of the reasons I am no longer an architect. If you skimp on the last 5 per cent, your buildings might kill people.

It's much safer for the world that I'm an academic.

I compensate for my 95-percenter tendencies by collaborating. I like collaborating for many reasons, but the safety in numbers part of it is particularly appealing. I don't expect my collaborators to do the last 5 per cent for me (although some of them do, bless their hearts). No – much in the same way I do housework because I don't want my friends to think I'm a slob, when others are depending on me I will do the last 5 per cent quickly and properly, no matter how bored and irritated it makes me feel.

Without doubt my best work is done with people who are not 95-percenters, people like my friend Rachael Pitt. When I want to give up and say 'good enough' she holds my feet to the fire and makes me finish it. Properly. Rachael's diligence makes me realise I just don't care enough about that last 5 per cent to be truly brilliant at research. I just hope I am creative and interesting enough that she'll continue to forgive me for putting the commas in the wrong place in that damn reference list.

The internet abounds with articles warning of the perils of perfectionist thinking. PhD students are often warned that being a perfectionist is the very kiss of death for a timely completion. But there's a difference between being a perfectionist and being thorough, detail-focussed and concerned with the quality of the work you are doing – in other words, a 100-percenter.

So why does a 100-percenter get confused with a perfectionist? Here are two thoughts.

You take a long time to get going with your writing

There's an epic amount of literature on just about every topic you can imagine. While a perfectionist will sift through this literature endlessly, without making decisions, your 100-percenter is just taking their sweet time to digest it properly. While personally I'm a student of the 'writing is thinking/thinking is writing' school of thought, I recognise not all people work that way. Some people just like to think and don't necessarily need to write a lot to do this.

If you haven't produced a single word towards your thesis in the last six months, you might have a problem, but if you have been reading, scribbling notes and feel like you are understanding some stuff, there's probably no real cause for concern. Here's a little test: talk to someone other than your supervisor about your topic. If you could bore for your country on your topic at a party, you are a 100-percenter. Tell people who label you a perfectionist that you are a Thinker – and then tell them to go away.

You care about getting it 'right', not necessarily getting it done on time

While your 95-percenter friend has done four conference papers this year, you've been toiling away with no visible results – yet. Despite diligent application of bottom to seat, your lack of publications makes you feel … inadequate. You are starting to get worried that you aren't 'productive', or living up to expectations, even though no one has actually told you what these expectations are.

If you find yourself becoming anxious when comparing yourself to other people, just stop.

What progress looks like for you will be different than what it looks like for others. Here's another test: write down a list of things that count as 'progress' in the last month or two: insights, ideas you've had, some data you've collected, analysis started – whatever counts as moving the project along. Do you have at least three items on the list? Then relax.

While I do think that perfect is the enemy of done, the last 5 per cent, as tedious as it is, is worth doing right because in the end it's the last 5 per cent that separates a good academic from a hack. And no one wants to be a hack.

●●● RESEARCHER, ORGANISE THYSELF

Recently I put together a promotion application. For those of you unfamiliar with the Australian system, this is similar to a tenure application in the US. You must compile everything you have done in your academic career, assess its impact and present it all as a legible 'story' of your contribution to your discipline and your university. Gathering evidence of your achievements and impact involves hours of combing databases to find convincing statistics, asking colleagues to write testimonials and reading back over your diary to remember what you did and when.

This turned out to be an intense month. I only had time to do promotion application work at night. I had to use my full range of emotional coping strategies: whingeing to Mr Thesis Whisperer (and anyone else who would stand still long enough to listen), chocolate, James Blunt albums on repeat, and so on. Slowly, painfully, I managed to compile and write the narrative of my academic self. This was a good thing to be forced to do. My academic CV now is a complete record of everything I have done in a format that is easy to update. As a bonus, I was reminded just how many friends I have in this industry.

Colleagues offered advice, sympathy and testimonials that brought tears to my eyes. Special shout out to Susan Mayson, Sandra West and Megan McPherson, who read drafts, and to the steadfast Mr Thesis Whisperer, who did a painstaking copyedit at 11 pm, right on the deadline. But I'm not here to talk about the promotions process (that's a story for another time) – I want to tell you what I learned about organising all the stuff we researchers make so you can write the story of you. Had I bothered to think about keeping track more carefully years ago I would have saved myself hours of frustration (and James Blunt albums).

An academic resume should be treated as a constantly evolving work in progress, not something you produce under pressure of a looming deadline. Most of the stuff I needed was on my laptop hard drive or the internet, but my computer is a bit like Thesis Whisperer Jnr's teenager bedroom. My digital stuff was strewn everywhere: stuffed in the wrong drawer, hiding under the bed or rotting, like a forgotten banana in a lunchbox. Not only was my own digital 'room' messy, bits of 'me' were stashed online everywhere – Google, Dropbox, academia.edu and various other sites. Don't be like me, OK? Researcher – organise thyself.

Here are some ideas to get you started.

Use your digital memory

I fly around the world, giving keynotes, presentations and workshops at other universities. Colleagues advised me that this is a mark of peer esteem and I was told to list in my CV the date, location and title of every single guest lecture or workshop. Retrieving the details from my electronic diary took a lot longer than it should have because I didn't realise when I started flying around for academic purposes that I would need the information later, and it was a mess.

Your diary will also contain the details you need to prove you have performed 'service' to your discipline and university community. This is stuff like sitting on committees, consultations, peer reviews, grant evaluations, editing work, organising events and so on. I have done a ton of stuff over the years, but I rarely, if ever, wrote it down.

Use whatever system you like, but think of your diary as a way to record everything you do for other people, no matter how insignificant it seems at the time. If you want to be super-organised, attach the script and/ or PowerPoint of your invited presentations to your diary entries and be consistent with naming, so you can search effectively. Better still, use a proper task manager like OmniFocus or Trello. Your computer has a better memory than you – use it properly and making a list of service activities and compiling evidence of peer esteem will be a breeze.

Choose your digital 'warehouse'

There are many ways to store your research papers and CV online: Academia.edu, LinkedIn, ResearchGate … Which one will still be there in ten years time? Who knows. We are in a pre-Facebook era in academic social network terms. It's far from clear which service is the Next Big Thing and which will end up being Betamaxed.

While we wait to see which service wins the academic social media arms race, I recommend you pick one you always keep up to date. Index your completed papers on a reference manager like EndNote, upload to your primary social media site and use this as a 'warehouse' to populate the other sites when you have time.

For what it's worth, I use LinkedIn for this purpose because the talent acquisition specialists hang out there (I am always open to potential job offers!).

File by activity

Where do I even start with electronic filing? No system is perfect, but for some time I've been following guidelines set out by David Allen in his classic book *How to Get Things Done*. Allen recommends filing by activity, which I've found is marginally better than any other system. My file system has a couple of folders in the root directory:

- ANU
- Presentations
- Research
- Teaching
- Supervision
- Thesis Whisperer
- Writing.

Inside each of these folders I have a folder for each year, and that's it. A relatively flat file structure means stuff doesn't get lost in some long-forgotten digital pocket. If I can't remember when I made a file, or can't find it by name, at least I know where to tell the computer to look for it.

If someone is nice to you in writing, keep it

It's well known in marketing circles that customer testimonials have coercive power. What better way to tell someone how great you are than to use other people's words? Hey, if they take the time to send it to you in an email, even better. Thank them nicely and put it in your feedback file. Even if you don't use their words, you'll remember who your supporters are and can chase them up for a glowing testimonial when the time comes.

Make your peace with the h-index

One day you'll have to demonstrate the 'impact' of your work. The most common way to do this is to look at citations your papers have attracted. The measure that's often used is the 'h-index'. The h-index has been criticised for being deeply flawed, but if a number is there, people will use it.

My h-index is four, which will sound low to those of you in the sciences. That's because the h-index is built for disciplines that publish short papers, not books and lengthy essays. To put my relatively low h-index in context, I benchmarked myself against other scholars in my discipline and school. I was heartened to learn that, despite all the time I have 'wasted' on blogging, I was average for someone already at the level I was aspiring to. One influential professor, after 30 years of publishing, had an h-index of nine. While I was doing this benchmarking I noticed how few of my colleagues had a Google Scholar page, which automagically generates your h-index for you. I just can't understand why people would neglect this useful scholarly 'brag wall'. It's easy enough to create one if you have published something and have a university address.

There are some thoughts to get you started, anyway. Have a think about how you will research the story of you when the time comes – your future self will thank you.

THESIS PRISON

One of my friends got pregnant twice during her doctorate and had a longer journey than most. While we raised a glass to her recent graduation I asked how it felt to be done.

'Liberating!' she said, 'But the last three months was hell. No one avoids that bit, right?'

I nodded emphatically. No matter how well you plan, there's bound to be a period of time where getting the thesis done will dominate your life. A thesis is a long-drawn-out project with many stages. Many of us have to go back to a full-time job before it's entirely finished. Still more of us study part-time from the very beginning and have to juggle multiple commitments the whole time. The hellish last part will temporarily squeeze out all the other things that normally keep you sane. Exercise, socialising, *The Good Wife* TV marathons

… all get cut in order to make way for the thesis. It's a bit like shrink-wrapping your life so that only the boring working bits are left. Working on your thesis feels like putting your head in a bucket at this point, but you just have to do it. After about a month or so you can feel like you are in Thesis Prison playing scrabble with the warden. It's a rare person who doesn't get a bit stir-crazy.

Recently I started counting calories and running in an effort to lose my 'baby weight' (I should add – my baby is now 13 and taller than me). Over a couple of months I have lost a dress size, but I often felt like I was back in Thesis Prison. So here are four tips for getting fit and/or surviving Thesis Prison.

Put on your damn shoes

Even though we all know that having a routine is valuable, sticking to it is much easier said than done. Although I've come to enjoy running, I almost always don't really want to do it. But if I put on my running shoes I know I will eventually force myself to go because I've started the process. Routines are largely about process: small actions done in a certain order. So just sit down at your desk and start doing something. Anything. Try some small but necessary tasks: good examples are filing and tagging references in your database, cleaning and formatting data, copyediting, etc. Work your way up to doing some writing. Conversely, just open your document anywhere and pick a place to start writing. Tell yourself that you can always throw it out if it's crap.

It's all about time served

Nobody even noticed my lifestyle changes until I'd lost nearly 10 kilograms, which took around three months. Most of the time I just felt like I was missing out on all the cake and getting nowhere. Similarly, Thesis Prison can be disheartening because progress is often invisible. It's possible to spend a whole day at your desk and feel like you have achieved nothing. One solution is to visualise the progress somehow. If I weigh myself once a week or measure my waist I can see the progress. I use the running apps on my phone to measure distance travelled and calories consumed. Likewise, when I was doing my thesis I stuck a piece of graph paper on the wall next to me and charted my progress by colouring in a block for every 1000 words. We follow a similar principle in our Thesis Boot Camps, where we hand out squeezy Lego-style blocks for every 5000 words written. It sounds silly, but it works.

Don't, whatever you do, compare yourself to the other runners

When you're a runner, you get to know the other people running in your neighbourhood. There was one woman whom I started to think of as the Queen of Running. She always looked immaculate and barely seemed to raise a sweat as she lapped me easily in the local park. I stared at her enviously as I huffed around the track, feeling like death warmed up. Compared to the Queen of Running I felt like a faker and totally inadequate. Then one day a friend stopped me on campus to say she'd seen me out on my run and complimented me on my technique, saying I 'looked like a pro'. She insisted I had inspired her to start running (presumably because if I could do it anyone could) and asked me if I could give her some tips.

I was astonished. I just assumed I looked the way I felt on the inside while I was running. The lesson? Thesis Prison distorts your perception of yourself. Everyone is running their own race. Just concentrate on winning yours.

Change it up

Running can be boring, so it's necessary to change the route often and spend money on whole new playlists and outfits (that's my excuse, anyway).

Writing can be really boring, so try a diagram or a matrix to progress your writing in different formats. A matrix is a way to play with your thoughts and see if you can make connections between ideas. Draw up a simple grid, or use a program like MS Word or Excel. On the left write a series of questions down the first column. Write the names of the papers you are reading in the top row. Then fill in each of the cells with how the paper addresses, or enlightens you on, the question in that row. A matrix is a helpful aid to writing because, while it forces some hierarchy on your thoughts, it frees you up from having to make transitions or think about what order ideas should be presented in an argument.

A more drastic solution is to take yourself to a new location where you have no choice but to write.

I'm glad to have escaped Thesis Prison by graduating, but sometimes I wonder if I really did. What no one tells you is that Thesis Prison is a state of being that occurs regularly in the life of a working academic. Large projects always require at least some time spent with your head in a bucket – but don't tell people who are finishing their thesis that!

 ENDNOTE VS ... EVERYTHING ELSE

Just before I handed in my thesis two things happened which up to then I had thought were PhD student urban myths:

1   A whole journal came out full of articles that 'scooped' my thesis topic (gah!).
2   EndNote bugged out and turned all my 400-odd references into gibberish (instant coronary!).

My supervisor solved crisis number one during a single phone call. 'It's a good thing, Inger,' he said cheerfully. 'Just point out in the introduction that the journal was published after you finished and this is evidence that the topic is hot.'

Mischief managed. (This strategy works really well, by the way, even if you don't have to employ it out of desperation.) The EndNote problem was a doozy, though. None of the students on the PhD floor at the University of Melbourne had experienced anything like it. Those who eyeballed my tattered thesis looked horrified. I could read their thoughts: 'Thank god this isn't me!' Believe me when I say this does not make the person facing an EndNote disaster feel any calmer.

Frantic calls to the library resulted in pointers to some helpful material, which failed completely to describe the exact problem. In the end, my mad Google skills led me to an obscure EndNote support forum. On it was a post which detailed the problem I was having, but the posted answer didn't work for me. I put out a cry for help on the same forum and crossed my fingers. Overnight a kind soul answered and fixed my problem. Thank you, internet! But no thank you, EndNote, you failed me in my hour of need. Up to that point I loved you, but now it was time to break up.

I'd heard rumours there were better reference managers out there, so I got my thesis handed in and looked around for an alternative solution. These days I would just ask Twitter, but, back then, accessing this kind of information was more random. A photocopied flyer, which my friend Scott Mayson picked up in a seminar room, led me to Mendeley. Unlike EndNote, Mendeley was easy to learn because it works in a similar way to iTunes. You can make a 'playlist' for each topic and it's social, so you can share your reference data with others. Your data is in the cloud, so no more data sticks and version control issues. The interface is lovely and clean, which was an unexpected bonus (I think it's a pity that the aesthetics of functional academic programs don't often get that kind of treatment). I spent a day or so transferring my data and loved the way it renamed all my PDFs in a consistent format at the press of a button. Being a social, sharing kind of person I put together a research education bibliography and linked it to the blog. I made an open Twitter literature list, added a few references and published it on the web. I woke up the next morning to find that many kindly souls had posted new references to it.

Instant literature searching? Sign me up!

I was captivated. I spoke with enthusiasm to all my friends about my new toy, trying to lure them away from the EndNote mothership. But, like so many intense love affairs, the lustre eventually wore off and my eye began to wander. Once you have loved and lost a reference manager, it is so much easier to move on. I was transferring my writing practice into Scrivener at that point, and people on Twitter told me that cite-while-you-write referencing worked better with Zotero. The key feature of Zotero is the way it integrates with the Firefox web browser, plus cloud storage, open source development, sharing, automatic metadata scraping ... oh – and it's free. What's not to love?

Well, I tried Zotero for a couple of months and, to be honest with you, I just couldn't warm to it. After the aesthetic and functional design of Mendeley, Zotero felt unnecessarily hard to use. I never did quite work out how to synch it properly. I quickly tired of fighting with the interface. I know many people love Zotero, but it was not for me. It seemed that Zotero was destined to be my rebound reference manager love affair. It was time to settle down and get married. All this moving around was hurting my paper kids. My digital life needed some order and routine so I turned again to Twitter with my wish list for a new reference manager. The wish list read:

- easy-to-use interface
- compatibility with Scrivener
- good search functions and ability to keep notes
- the ability to auto-populate fields with metadata from PDFs
- the cloud.

My friend Andrew Van Der Stock suggested I try Papers2 for the Mac. It had everything I wanted but the cloud, which didn't seem like a deal-breaker. While Zotero and Mendeley were free, Papers2 was $80, but there was a free trial for a month. Papers2 had a great search function, combined with note taking and highlighting capacities. It is wonderful at scraping metadata from PDFs and populating fields like author and publisher. Often these are not properly done in the first place (honestly – I really do wonder what we pay those journal publishers for). If Papers2 doesn't get the fields quite right you can ask it to search the web and find a match. With the help of my friend Jason Downs I discovered other cool features such as the ability to set up a proxy and search databases like Google Scholar from within the interface, which enables me to import from the web, seamlessly, with one click.

In other words, I was happy to settle down with Papers2 and have subsequently upgraded to Papers3. I offer this story because it illustrates how choosing the right reference manager is deeply personal and contingent on a whole lot of factors. Sometimes I yearn for other features, but the more I get to know Papers, the more I appreciate its trusty and efficient design. Deep, lasting love is always like that, at least so I've found.

SHUT UP AND WRITE!

In early 2010 I had a phone conversation with my friend Ben Kraal, who showed me his excellent and funny *Brown Car Blog*. I got nerdishly excited about the potentials of social media and crowd-sourced social research. Camera + internet connection + a place to store and share images has turned mobile phones into the ideal data collection instrument: hello, ethnographic fun! Ben and I started to toss around some ideas for a photoblog theme and came up with a research question to drive it: Does the food get better the closer to the Vice-Chancellor you get?

Of course, it's a rather silly research question, but being serious wasn't the point of the exercise, which was just to play around with the phone. However, there was an immediate benefit of choosing food for an ethnographic study. As long as I kept people out of the pictures I didn't have to seek research ethics approval (that food was at risk of being eaten anyway). I started with a Tumblr blog called *Refreshments Will Be Provided*, which enabled me to make my data collection open to contributions from others. Quite a few people, mostly PhD students, have been so kind as to submit photos. Later I moved the project onto Instagram, introducing the hashtag #refreshmentswillbeprovided as a way for people to share their contributions. As a result I was able to develop a bigger and more interesting data set which doesn't just reflect my own corner of the academic world.

After six or so years of continuous data collection, I feel confident to declare that the answer to our research question is 'yes': the more lofty the academic company, the fancier the snacks. While collecting this data on food I discovered a number of interesting things, but the most immediately fascinating observation was how much of my own academic work gets carried out in cafes. I write, read, take notes, think and meet people in cafes on and off campus on an almost daily basis. I am such a regular at one cafe on campus that it's really my second office. Recognising the value of this kind of 'free range' academic practice, together with my colleagues Jonathan O'Donnell and Tseen Khoo (of the *Research Whisperer* blog), we started a regular 'Shut Up and Write!' session at RMIT University, based on the cafe novel writing meet-ups my sister Anitra had encountered in San Francisco. We talked about it on our blogs and on Twitter and before we knew it, a global movement had begun.

'Shut Up and Write!' turns writing from a solitary to a social experience. The concept is simple: meet up with others in a cafe (hopefully one with plenty of power points), and write. The concept originated in the San Francisco Bay Area, among creative writers, but, thanks to social media, has spread among research students around the world. The idea is to make the act of writing fun and relaxing, as the San Francisco group puts it: 'No critiquing, exercises, lectures, ego, competition or feeling guilty'. Anyone can start a 'Shut Up and Write!' group – you don't need permission or any extra resources, but we have found it works best if you:

- Meet at a regular, pre-arranged time. This means there is not a lot of organisational work required, so long as one person commits to turn up at the assigned time and greet new members. You might want to share this duty with another person so it doesn't become onerous.

- Create a contact point for new members. This can be someone's email, or a social media presence such as a Facebook page, which acts as a rallying point. Some groups even make posters advertising their sessions and put them up around campus.

- Keep the writing sprints short. Use the Pomodoro Technique (a 25-minute stretch of focussed concentration). Between the pomodoros, take as much time as the group would like to drink hot beverages, talk and eat. Have one person willing to act as 'Pomodoro Chief' who will do time calls (there are many free apps which you can use to keep time).

- Work on anything, so long as it's work – transcription, analysis, reading, organising your notes, even email (although I don't recommend it). No exercises or judgment, remember? The only rule is to be silent when everyone else is.

- Accept that 'Shut Up and Write!' is not for everyone. Some people may only come once; others will be regulars. If no one else turns up, 'Shut Up and Write!' is almost as much fun on your own (it's nice to work somewhere other than the office every now and then).

- Remember, it doesn't just have to be PhD students who do it. Early career academics, professional staff and others need to put time aside for writing too. It's the perfect opportunity to create cross-institutional links – you might even want to be open to people from other universities coming along.

I hear about new 'Shut Up and Write!' groups starting all the time. While it's not for everyone, students from around the world tell me that this is the perfect environment for them to write in. Isn't it odd that these noisy, busy spaces seem conducive to research writing and reading? Especially when you consider that the primary reason academics resist open-plan offices is that the presence of other people is distracting. What is going on?

I wondered aloud on Twitter about this contradiction and got a number of interesting replies. @LizDobsonUoH pointed out that such a practice has a proud heritage: JK Rowling famously wrote the Harry Potter series in a cafe. @RebeccaRDamari sent me an extremely funny and interesting article in the *New York Times* in which a reporter describes his visit to a particularly famous cafe where 'Laptops had colonized every flat surface. No one uttered a word; people just stared into screens, expressionless. It felt like that moment in a horror movie when the innocent couple stumbles into a house filled with hibernating zombies, and they listen, in terror, as the floorboard creaks.'*

@idreamofcodeine described her motives for occupying cafes as stemming from 'a desire to appear studious to those around you'. @orientalhotel expressed similar motivations and added: 'I think cafe time allows me to focus on just one thing w/o pressure to feel I should read 10 books/websites at once'. @shannonej remarked: 'As a social person a cafe is a social setting but I'm not interacting so work gets done. In a quiet office I get distracted.' @misskatielow agreed and pointed out the importance of caffeine in this process. @ailsa pointed out that you are 'off the grid' when you are in a cafe – unless you take a call, no one has to know you are there.

I started to wonder about the complex relationship between noise and distraction. I talked to a friend of mine who has adult ADHD who told me how much working in front of the television helped her to concentrate. Reading the list of ADHD symptoms on Wikipedia was a bit confronting, I have to say – I could certainly tick off a few, especially the 'inattentive' ones:

---

* David Sax, 'Destination: Laptopistan', *New York Times*, 3 December 2010.

- being easily distracted, missing details, forgetting things, and frequently switching from one activity to another
- having difficulty maintaining focus on one task
- becoming bored with a task after only a few minutes, unless doing something enjoyable
- not seeming to listen when spoken to.

Maybe my addiction to cafes is a coping strategy for academic ADHD, but, you know, with caffeine. I reckon that makes it ok.

HOW TO LOOK CLEVERER THAN YOU ACTUALLY ARE

Not so long ago I missed a flight back home from Sydney. When I realised I was eating dinner instead of being on a plane on the way home to my family I flipped out. Luckily I was with the wonderful Mary-Helen Ward, who made me take some deep breaths and finish my sausages while she looked up the number for the airline. When I finally got through to a person at the call centre the conversation went something like this:

Call centre worker: It says here 'Dr Mewburn' – is that correct?

Me: That's right.

Call centre worker: And why is it that you missed your flight, Dr Mewburn?

Me: I misread the ticket.

(A short pause – I could feel the confusion down the phone line.)

Call centre worker: How did you misread the ticket?

Me: Look, I only have a PhD, OK? It doesn't make me immune from stupid.

Sadly, this is true. A PhD involves an ability to learn new things and a certain amount of gritty determination, but it doesn't make you immune from stupid. If anything, getting a PhD makes you more aware of your limitations than you were before. The more you know, the more you know you don't know – if you know what I mean.

I'm privileged to work with some extraordinarily

intelligent people. I mean, really clever – intimidatingly clever. Clever to the point where I dare not open my mouth in some meetings for fear someone will discover I shouldn't really be there. It's not easy to live in a university and be of average intelligence, so I have made a study of how clever people behave in order to imitate them. The general principle here is: if I act like a clever person, I may become clever – or at least I will appear to be clever (which, existentially speaking, is the same thing).

Here are five of my best strategies.

Wherever possible, speak last

When I first started going to 'grown-up' university meetings I would immediately jump in and give my opinion as soon as the room fell silent. I think this was a hangover from my school days. I was the nerdy girl at the front of the class, always out to prove that I was smarter than anyone else. However, monopolising the conversation just doesn't work in the professional world – it comes across as annoying, especially if you are a woman. I rage against this fact, of course, but strategic silence can be used to your advantage.

Speaking last gives you a position of temporary power in a conversation. I have tested this strategy for years and found it to be sound. If you wait and listen carefully to what others are saying it gives you time to reflect on and digest the conversation. If you speak last, you are more likely to be the one who comes up with the unexpected, novel or creative suggestion, rather than just stating the obvious. If you can't think of something creative, speaking last gives you the opportunity to connect what other people are saying and offer an explanation or overriding principle. Happily, when you do this, others in the meeting will usually agree because it was their idea anyway.

Instant cleverness guaranteed.

Have some 'pocket facts' handy

As Mr Thesis Whisperer is fond of saying, the plural of anecdote is not data. Throwing a few choice statistics about your field of expertise into a conversation will make you look extremely clever, without effort. I have lost count of the number of times I have sat in meetings where someone says that such-and-such must be true about doing a research degree because it was true for them, or because they have heard the 'fact' repeated so often. Statements like 'Research students are poor communicators and need to be taught transferable skills' drive me crazy, so I try to have some 'pocket facts' on hand to counter these common assumptions.

Recently my friend Nigel Palmer did an analysis

which showed that most research students think they bring skills to their PhD, not the other way around. The only skill that students consistently claim they developed while studying for a PhD is library and information retrieval skills. This shouldn't surprise us because 55 per cent of students come to research degree study from the workplace, not from undergraduate degrees, and a significant number of them have had a gap of more than ten years since they last studied. That little statistic usually stops that particular line of criticism of research students dead.

You're welcome.

Learn the lingo

Every place I have ever worked or studied has had its own dialect. At RMIT University we were extraordinarily fond of acronyms. Here's a list of the ones I used on an almost daily basis: ATN, DDoGS, RTS, TEQSA, AQF, DIISR, DEEWR, PREQ, CES, DVC (R&I).

And that's not counting the more esoteric ones, which I recognise but don't use often. Mr Thesis Whisperer calls these 'TLAs' (three-letter acronyms). TLAs populate most advanced knowledge fields and institutions. Sadly, knowing the right TLAs – specifically, what they mean and how they relate to each other – makes you look clever. Luckily, acquiring this sort of information is a bit like learning to spell: you only have to learn it once. If you have a decent memory, which most academics do, a little bit of effort here will make you look clever for years and years.

Beware of jargon

Knowing your TLAs is advantageous, but if you speak in jargon too much the truly clever people will get suspicious. There's an excellent chapter in Howard Becker's book *Writing for Social Scientists* in which he talks about the urge to 'write classy'. I guess we do this from a sense of inferiority, but you can't just copy language you see in books and papers and think it makes you appear more intelligent.

I have absolutely no data to back this up, but in my experience of university life, most academics are not going to admit they don't understand you when you use impenetrable jargon, they just won't really listen to you (or cite your papers). People who can translate difficult concepts into language that others can understand are more likely to be persuasive. Since persuasiveness is often conflated with cleverness, speaking clearly and concisely is a winning strategy. In my view, this is as true for thesis writing as it is for meetings and presentations.

Turn the problem around

Sometimes problems need simple solutions, not more complex ones. One trick which my old boss Denise Cuthbert shared with me is to ask: 'What should we do less of?'. A disarmingly simple question, but an extremely powerful one. Take your work day as one example: what can you do less of? Does more time spent mean better results? I've found that working in shorter bursts, but with more focus and concentration, can help you achieve more than sitting at your desk all day banging your head on the screen.

———————

None of this helps me catch a flight on time, mind you. Sadly, the sausage dinner incident isn't an isolated one, but when it comes to committee meetings – it's so handled.

 # A VISIT FROM THE PROCRASTINATION FAIRY

Not long after I finished my PhD I sent a paper to the top journal in my field containing my thesis results. The editor wanted to publish it, but demanded significant changes. All to the good, of course – there's a reason it's a top journal – but I found the process of revisiting my thesis incredibly hard work. In fact, it would be fair to say that the Procrastination Fairy sprinkled me with her Can't Be Bothered Dust in a big way. Revising my thesis was a profoundly unpleasant activity. The problem with a peer review, if properly applied, is that it leads to DOUBT. To some extent I lost confidence in the work and started to second-guess myself. As a consequence, every time I opened the documents I felt an uncomfortable sense of failure. It was easy – far too easy – just not to open the documents in the first place. The problem of procrastination can reach critical levels before I will do anything about it.

Sadly, this was not the only time I have been dosed with the Can't Be Bothered Dust. Some time ago, ANU gave me a chance to make a MOOC. For those of you not in the know, MOOC stands for 'massive open online course'. The MOOC would allow thousands of people to participate in this ANU course from around the world, for free. The process of bidding to run a MOOC at ANU is by competitive tender, so I was surprised when I was given special funding to do one. It was an honour to be singled out and jump the queue, so to speak. It showed that ANU management had pleasing faith in my abilities …

Hmmm.

Should they really have so much faith?

In less than an hour I had convinced myself that ANU management had made a big mistake. Sure, I had run a successful blog for years, and authored more than a few online courses, but this was different. I'd never done anything on this scale before. I convinced myself it was going to be a miserable failure. The pressure to perform freaked me right out. I felt like I'd been asked to organise a massive party on a global scale. What if no one enrolled? Not only would I fail, but EVERYONE IN THE WORLD WOULD SEE ME FAIL. The whole world would discover what I had known, secretly, for a long time … that I am only pretending to be clever and interesting.

I've seen this pattern of thinking, which is called the imposter syndrome, in PhD students many times, but it took me a surprisingly long time to recognise it in myself. After (metaphorically) smacking myself upside the head a few times, I applied the imposter syndrome cure I always recommend to others. I decided to suspend judgment and just get on with it – there was time to worry about whether it was any good later. I tried to write down ideas, *any* ideas – bad ideas, stupid ideas … I worked on ideas for nearly a year, but made frustratingly slow progress. I had what golfers call 'the yips' – a sudden and unexplained lack of ability, just when I needed it most.

As the yips dragged on, and on, the fear started to set in. Everything I wrote seemed dumb, boring, pointless. ANU got a bit worried about me for real at this point, and a couple of people were assigned to help. Talking with generous, open-minded colleagues was just what I needed. Katie and Chris listened to my troubles and encouraged me to see these as the themes for the MOOC. We worked together to reorientate the MOOC around the effects of emotions on research student performance and eventually (after much debate) called it 'How to Survive Your PhD'. We imagined 'How to Survive Your PhD' as a node in a huge global conversation, where students and supervisors could, together, work to understand the emotional problems that can get in the way of good research progress, and find and share new strategies for coping. We found ways for the conversation to spill into other spaces – social media and campus coffee shops; supervisors' offices and classrooms. At a certain point we realised that we had a massive, global, free platform – why confine the conversation to the university? We thought of all the mothers, fathers, brothers, sisters and partners who might want to join in the conversation. Many of these people are heavily invested in the success of their loved ones. So I tore up what I had and rewrote it in plain language so it was accessible to anyone who was genuinely interested in helping PhD students survive and thrive.

Long story short, the MOOC was a raving success. Over 13 000 people enrolled and, to my surprise, around 18 per cent of those who started finished it – six times more than we had expected.

You'd think that after this experience I would get over myself, learn to feel the fear and do it anyway, but oh, no, no, no. The next large project was this book. The very generous editors at NewSouth Publishing were happy for me to compile posts and call it done, but for a year I mucked around with various formats, trying to stitch posts together and hating the results. Then a well-meaning soul pointed out that a book has reviewers, whereas a blog has fans, and the fear took hold. Then the Procrastination Fairy dusted me but good. I didn't open the file for six months and the more I procrastinated about it, the worse the fear of failure got. I seriously considered voiding the contract – a contract that was a dream offer to write anything I wanted. The only thing that cured me was talking to a lot of people, potential readers and colleagues, all of whom encouraged me to get over myself and just do it. Mr Thesis Whisperer offered a lot of support and quietly put coffees by my elbow as I spent weekend mornings and holiday time up to my elbows in editing. I employed various other coping methods (James Blunt on repeat, chocolate, cat videos) and eventually it was done.

There's lots of advice out there on the subject of

procrastination – in fact, one can do some really good procrastinating just reading the advice. It was while doing this that I came across a great article on procrastination in the *New Yorker* by James Surowiecki, which was an extended review on an academic book on the topic of procrastination called *The Thief of Time*. In the succinctly titled 'Later',* Surowiecki argues that procrastination can be seen as the 'quintessential modern problem' and that academics are prone to procrastination, perhaps because of the largely self-directed nature of our work. I'm not sure this is the only reason, but the perils of procrastination are legion and best discussed at pleasantly procrastinater-ly coffees with colleagues.

The fundamental problem with procrastination is that telling yourself that procrastination is a stupid thing to do doesn't help. We all know that the unpleasant sensations which arise from putting off an unpleasant (or boring) task can be as bad, even worse, than actually doing the task you were avoiding in the first place. As Surowiecki puts it, 'when we put off preparing for that meeting by telling ourselves that we'll do it tomorrow, we fail to take into account that tomorrow the temptation to put off work will be just as strong'.

This precisely explains my problem with revising those damn papers, the MOOC and this book. Every

---

* James Surowiecki, 'Later', *New Yorker*, 11 October 2011.

day I told myself that I would start tomorrow. Yet when tomorrow came the urge to delay starting was as strong as ever. My stories of procrastination show I need outside pressure to counteract the inner urge to put off the job. I suppose this is why the imposition of deadlines on PhD students is ultimately a good thing. Creating your own deadlines within candidature and agreeing on them with your supervisors is a good strategy for overcoming the urge to delay writing. A deadline is not the only kind of outside pressure available to you: living on a student income gets pretty intolerable after a couple of years too.

Deadlines are not the whole solution, of course. The curious nature of procrastination was captured well in another line from Surowiecki's article: 'we often procrastinate not by doing fun tasks but by doing jobs whose only allure is that they aren't what we should be doing'. The truth of this struck deeply. I am currently doing research which involves reading policy documents from every other university and putting their key points in a matrix. A more excruciatingly boring research task I can barely think of – yet I will happily do it rather than write this book. Maybe the secret is to stay with the feelings about the work, not just on the rational reasons why the work must be done. With this book, the key was to find a way to start feeling a sense of anticipation, instead of dread; a way to ignite that spark of interest and curiosity in the work itself so I *want* to do the work.

The final thought of Surowiecki's I want to share is the most powerful: procrastination may stem from the nature of identity. We like to think of ourselves as unified selves, but according to Surowiecki we are 'different beings, jostling, contending, and bargaining for control'. In other words, everyone is made up of 'multiple selves' who want different things. My 'want to get a published book out' self is in constant struggle with my other selves: my 'want to have coffee', 'want to read Twitter', 'want to write for the blog' and 'want to empty my email inbox' selves – just to name a few. I am also different from my past self. Past Self sets a time in the diary when the work should be done, but Future Self can develop oppositional defiance disorder and refuse to comply. My 'want to get published' self will always be at a disadvantage compared to those selves who have more intrinsically interesting – and easy to satisfy – desires. The trick then is to think of what kind of bargain I can make with my 'want to have coffee' self which will enable me to open those files ...

I might think about that while I go and have a coffee.

💬 WHERE DO GOOD IDEAS COME FROM?

A PhD thesis or dissertation is supposed to make 'a significant and original contribution to knowledge'. The PhD is a way of learning how to create new knowledge through technique and method, but we pay little attention to the creativity that's required to make the whole shebang work. It's assumed you just know how to be creative; that it's an intrinsic characteristic possessed by researchers, not a set of techniques like the rest of the thesis process. The problem with this way of thinking is that it presumes you can't get better at it. It's better to think of creativity as a set of processes and procedures, not a quality you either have or don't.

You'll search in vain for a good primer on how to be a creative researcher. In their classic *How to Get a PhD*, Estelle Phillips and Derek Pugh set out 16 ways to be original (page 62 of the current edition, if you are interested), but they don't say anything about how to come up with the original ideas in the first place. Similarly, while *Doctorates Downunder* has chapters full of useful suggestions for managing your time and enriching your study experience, which may increase your chances of finishing your doctorate, they don't tackle the topic of being original. Don't get me wrong – it is good to know what originality means in relation to doing a PhD, but it's far better to know what you have to do to produce enough original ideas to fill a thesis.

The reason why so many books avoid this topic, perhaps rightly, is that creativity is assumed to be a disciplinary issue or an individual matter. Either you know enough about your subject to see the way to produce novel ideas, or you are a naturally creative person who will come up with them anyway. But is this really the case? Are there actions you can take that can help you come up with more ideas and solutions to research problems – regardless of discipline?

One intriguing approach is to consider the role of community in creativity. In the paper 'Social origins of good ideas', sociologist Ronald Burt tackles just this problem. Burt explored the production and uptake of good ideas in a supply chain logistics company by exploring the nature of discussion networks among managers. He found that the network in the company was characterised by a 'bridge and cluster' formation. Most people work in clusters, only discussing ideas with their immediate work colleagues (within clusters). Relatively few people would act as 'bridgers', talking through ideas with colleagues in multiple clusters. Managers who had a diverse social network, who 'bridged' between clusters of smaller discussion networks, were 'at risk of having more good ideas'. He supports this argument with a whole bunch of numbers which seem pretty convincing to me. Now, I could probably drive a truck through this method on the grounds that he doesn't really take into account the influence of materiality, such as physical objects and locations, and how they give shape to relations between people. You might question how generalisable this knowledge is, given that a logistics company is bound to have some unique constraints. But I think the findings are interesting nonetheless.

The hypothesis which lies behind this work is that, within a discussion cluster, information, beliefs and behaviours tend to become more homogeneous over time. This is certainly a phenomenon you'll see if you work for any period of time in the same office, or within a family group for that matter. Burt argues that 'bridgers' discuss ideas with a wide range of people, not just the ones closest to hand. As a consequence they are more likely to be exposed to contradictory ideas and alternative practices. If these bridgers are astute and thoughtful, they can see ways to transfer or combine ideas and approaches from elsewhere to their own problems. In effect, Burt claims, 'Creativity is an import–export business'. A mundane idea in one area can be a spectacular one in another. Burt argues that 'the certain path to being creative is to find a constituency more ignorant than yourself' and notes that this is a common tactic in academia (!).

Here's where it gets interesting for people doing a PhD – and working researchers, for that matter. Think about it for a moment: what do you spend most of your time doing? Probably doing experiments, making stuff, writing stuff and/or reading the work of others. Hopefully you will also be hanging out with your peers and talking to your supervisors. These are good ways of generating ideas, but is there more you could be doing?

One thing administrators and academics in my university constantly complain about is that it's hard to convince PhD students to attend lunchtime seminars put on by other researchers. When I was doing my PhD it always seemed like a waste of time to break my flow and attend such events unless I knew the person who was presenting, or the topic of the seminar seemed especially relevant. I always assumed that the discussion was unlikely to have any direct relevance – but now I wonder how much useful, indirect relevance I was missing out on. Listening to ideas that aren't directly relevant are opportunities to cross-breed exciting new idea hybrids.

Another sure creativity killer is to hold on too tightly to pre-existing ideas and try to avoid errors. The best way to illustrate the folly of this is through a couple of stories.

A friend of a friend did his PhD on the use of hormones to promote plant growth. The first part of the study involved growing a series of plants using a method published in an earlier paper. The method was meant to yield 15 new plants per round, but the plant researcher only got eight. Perplexed, he threw out his materials and tried again, only to get the same result. This time he assumed the temperature was wrong, threw out his materials and tried again. Once more: nothing. For a year he fiddled around, trying to get the expected 15 plants, but he never did. Later the plant researcher happened to go to a conference and meet the person who did the original study. He took the opportunity to describe his failures in exhausting detail and ask for help. The person who did the original study merely blinked and said 'Oh yes, that experiment didn't work particularly well'.

As it turned out, the original person never did get 15 plants using that method.

In other words, the original researcher lied.

It's tempting to view the PhD researcher in this story as a bit of an idiot for assuming he was doing something wrong, but this would overlook the fact that the written word can have immense persuasive power. And it's not just what is written on a page which can lead us researchers astray – it's the ideas which get stuck in our heads. For example, it is not uncommon for PhD students to turn up to our statistical consulting service asking the mathematicians to 'fix' their results, when the results are, in fact, correct. You would expect the students to be relieved to find out they did their analysis right, but apparently many will still insist the numbers must be wrong because they didn't 'fit' the hypothesis which was being tested.

We need preconceptions – let's call them hunches – to get going in the first place, but problems can develop when we hold on to them too tightly. I was reminded of this while working on a research project about PhD students and progress reports. Twice a year we ask our PhD students to fill in a progress report accounting for how they spent their time and what they will do next (you may have a similar system at your university). Administrators and supervisors complain that progress reporting is a meaningless 'rubber stamp' exercise that should be changed, or even abandoned, so we decided to study it and see what could be done.

Our focus groups confirmed that students felt the same way as the administrators and supervisors: the progress reporting procedure was largely meaningless. However, we were wrong in our assumption that students would want to change the system too. Many *liked* that it was a rubber stamp exercise. It seems the mere act of writing a plan can be psychologically reassuring and the administrative meaninglessness of the reports meant that no one would attack them when the plans didn't translate to reality. I puzzled over this until I realised that all our stakeholders were being pragmatic, but pragmatic meant something different to students. It didn't mean useful – it meant not at all useful. In retrospect this explanation was blindingly obvious, but it took an embarrassingly long time to come to me because I was thinking with my hunch, rather than looking at the data. Actually, I was thinking like an administrator, not a researcher (oh, the shame!).

Once I had become aware of this tendency to rely on my initial hunch, the rest of the analysis came easily. I just assumed that my first thought would be wrong and looked for other explanations.

We don't often think about how useful these kinds of errors can be – if they are taken seriously. In his book *Where Good Ideas Come From*, Steven Johnson makes some interesting observations on the nature of error and creativity, citing research on how people free associate from trigger words. Forty per cent of people presented with the word 'green' will say 'grass'; 80 per cent when shown the word 'blue' will suggest another colour, or say the word 'sky'. Only a few people will volunteer words like 'Ireland', 'leaves' or 'jeans'.

It would be easy to assume that the outliers are naturally more 'creative', but there's probably something more interesting going on. In another experiment, people were exposed to the colour blue while sitting in front of a screen with a group. The twist in this research design is the participants were unaware they were sitting in a room full of actors. The actors insisted that the blue colour on the screen was red, which was probably very confusing to the poor research participants. Later the same research participants were asked to do the free association activity. Interestingly, they produced more outlier words than the control group, who had not been sitting with actors. Perhaps this explains why humour and absurdity are so important in human cultures? (For me, this provides justification for watching stupid cat videos when I should be working).

There's certainly comfort in conforming with existing theories and ideas, rather than challenging them. It takes confidence to take 'wrong' results seriously, because you have to examine your own biases. If our hapless plant researcher had had more confidence in his own ability, he wouldn't have wasted a whole year. But I think his story shows us that confidence can sometimes be in short supply when you are doing your PhD.

Which leaves me with a final thought: does a lack of confidence stem, at least in part, from a fear of being examined or subjected to peer review? Perhaps in our heart of hearts we still view the examination of our work as a 'test' through which we have to pass, rather than a review process which ensures our work is the best that it can be? I'm not sure. In lieu of an answer I can only say: try to have confidence in your doubt – and doubt in your confidence!

I will finish with some questions for us to ponder.

How can you create an ideas 'import–export' business? How much time do you spend discussing ideas with others? Who are they? Do you need to find more people who will expose you to different ways of thinking and doing? Since no one likes a freeloader, what might people in these other areas learn from you?

PARENTING THROUGH A PHD: FIVE WAYS TO NOT GO INSANE

PhD students are an interesting cohort. At our university the average age of a PhD student is 36, which means many students have some family responsibilities, either to a spouse, elderly parents, children or animals. Parenting is challenging for PhD students because, in addition to the caring work that you have to do, there is huge potential for WORRY and GUILT. Children get sick, they fall over at school, get stung by bees, have problems with their playmates, stick coins so far up their nose that they have to have their stomach pumped … (that last one is true, by the way, and please don't ask why).

Added to this, parents must constantly have one eye on the future consequences of the actions they take today. In fact, you name an activity – a fun one – and there will be some expert out there who can tell you how bad it will be for your child and how much it will screw them up as an adult. You can't win, but you can try, so here are my top five tips for parenting through a PhD.

1. Embrace daycare

My son was eight months old when I started my Masters degree and seven years old when I finished my PhD. The poor little guy is probably the only kid at his school who knows that doctors don't just look after sick people. I was able to do this because of our wonderful daycare centre. As a woman I felt a lot of social pressure to not use daycare, but I resisted and I am so glad. As Hillary Clinton once said: It takes a village to raise a child. I'm no child-raising expert, but the daycare people who helped bring up Thesis Whisperer Jnr were. They patiently taught my son to eat with a spoon, drink from a cup, go to the toilet and dress himself, among many other things. They also helped him learn to manage his feelings, talk about them and make friends with others. As a result I think in many ways my son is more emotionally mature than I am or will ever be.

Daycare professionals helped me be a better parent. They gave me advice about toilet training, sleep issues and any number of funny rashes. When I was feeling like I was doing a crap job, they reassured me that everything was OK and that my son wouldn't turn into a serial killer. Oh – and they didn't have a television there, so he actually spent time making things, digging in the dirt and having all those educational experiences that I was too tired, or uncreative, to do with him myself. Which leads me to point two.

2. Neglect-o-trons are ok

Someone very wise and funny once called the TV an off switch for children. Certainly large amounts of my Masters and PhD were written using the electronic babysitter, or as my sister calls it, 'the neglect-o-tron'. I'm not proud of it, but that's the way it was, no point in denying it. I did assuage my guilt about TV time by forcing the poor child to watch mainly educational programs. Rather than spend a fortune on DVDs, we connected a computer to the TV so we could control what he watched (this was 15 years ago, mind you – way before there was a 'kids' setting on Netflix). Before he could read, this system worked well. After he could read, not so much. I would often come home to find he'd erased all my episodes of *Grand Designs* so he had room for *Scooby-Doo*.

3. Reach out to other PhD parents

The other PhD students with kids are usually instant friends – shared experiences and all that. If you are lucky and your kids like each other, there is potential for play dates and sleepovers. It's probably good for your kid to see that other kids have to put up with the presence of a PhD in their lives. Even if you only strike up work-place friendships, the benefits of a therapeutic moan with someone who knows what you are going through cannot be overestimated!

4. Be proud of what you do

I tried not to be apologetic about the time that the PhD took away from my family. I felt like this would send all kinds of bad messages to both partner and child. Whenever I had to say no to doing something on PhD-related grounds I would explain to my son that the PhD was important to the whole family, not just me. I was study-ing to make a difference to our future. A PhD meant a better job, a roof over his head, food in his mouth and other fun stuff.

I made sure to show him how much I liked PhD study. Some weekends I would take him in to my office and work for an hour or two, setting him up at his own desk with some 'work' for my PhD so he felt like he was helping. Then we would go out for cake and explore the campus while talking about what uni is like and why it is a great place to be. He still remembers these fun times and wants to do his own PhD, so it can't have been that traumatic.

5. Sometimes it's better to just give up

My son was three when the chickenpox vaccine came out. I trotted off to the doctors as soon as possible, only to be told that they were out of stock for two weeks. That very day the creche posted a sign saying that a child had been diagnosed.

Too late.

Brendan came out in lots and lots of spots. Naturally this happened right before a major milestone presentation, so I was stressed out. But Brendan clearly felt terrible. All he wanted to do was sit on my lap and watch *Toy Story* repeatedly for three days. I tried to read, but after the first day I went into some kind of stupor. It's hard to read Heidegger while listening to Buzz Lightyear arguing with Woody, so I just gave up. I sat there and cuddled him for three days and you know what? It was kind of beautiful.

 THE PERILS OF PHD PARENTING

Last week Thesis Whisperer Jnr (aged nine and three quarters) had to find out seven facts about Ireland for a school project. After the last homework debacle, where we ended up in a screaming match, I have made an effort to relax my PhD parenting style. So I set him up with the encyclopaedia and told him to get on with it while I did a bit of blog maintenance. After 20 minutes or so of mucking around he got out his pencil and started writing a list. I couldn't help myself and looked over at what he had written.

Ireland's flag is orange, white and green.

So far so good, I thought and looked at the next item on the list:

People in Ireland believe in Leprechauns.

The PhD monster inside me was roused; the words were out of my mouth before I could even think:

Me: What evidence do you have for that claim about everyone in Ireland believing in leprechauns?

TW Jnr: What?

Me: That's a blatant generalisation!

TW Jnr: Huh?

Me: Well … Do you believe in leprechauns?

TW Jnr: Um … no?

Me: Are boys who live in Ireland somehow different than you?

TW Jnr: Er … no?

Me: So do all boys in Ireland believe in leprechauns?

At this point Thesis Whisperer Jnr burst into tears, threw his pen down on the page and stormed off in a huff. Later, when we both calmed down, we had a little talk. It turned out that he had to illustrate the facts he had found. He included leprechauns as a 'fact' because, well, he wanted to draw a leprechaun.

I felt like a complete asshole.

Some time ago I wrote a post called Parenting through Your PhD, which was about trying to carve out time for study when you have a young child. I thought I would be able to balance my work time with family life when I finished my PhD, but sadly this is not the case. Becoming an academic is like signing up for a whole lifetime of homework. The time-management challenges are pretty much the same, but now you have a whole lot of education which affects your parenting in sometimes bizarre ways. Here are my top five perils of being a PhD parent.

You are the parent their teacher dreads talking to

I have a PhD in an education-related topic and, like many of you I'm sure, I have done a lot of teaching. Of course, my experience as a teacher does not include primary school–aged children, but this doesn't stop me from being obnoxiously opinionated. I am a complete nightmare at parent–teacher interviews and will spout post-structuralist theory on why our son can't spell until the teacher's eyes glaze over. I don't want to be like this, but it seems I am sadly compulsive. Luckily Mr Thesis Whisperer will kick me under the table when the four-syllable words start coming out of my mouth.

Your theories become their theories

I don't know how it happens, but your kids can soak up your academic theories along with your taste in music and politics. The other day my son, now aged 15, told me he was enjoying a novel because 'the narrative structure is inclusive because there are people who are same-sex attracted'. I do wonder how much he can talk about gender politics in the schoolyard. Sometimes your kid's knowledge of theoretical concepts can lead to conflict with the teacher, as @pinniesp explained to me on Twitter: 'when his teacher said Australia was discovered, he corrected him: "colonised". I felt a bit of remorse about the indoctrination – this may have been in year 7 – but oh well.'

Precision in all things

My son had to get used to substantiating his knowledge claims with evidence and deal with the fact that I am a grammar nerd. Having a parent who insists on the correct use of semicolons in a grade 4 essay is a complete drag, I'm sure. Other parents on Twitter told me that adult–child conflict over homework is even worse if you work with statistics, as @DrBekMarketing remarked: 'my kids hate it too when I go PhD-parent on them. Their response: 'n =1 is a sufficient sample size mum!'

Googling is not 'research'

On the tram the other day I heard a 16-year-old girl complaining to her mother about the bad mark on her essay. Apparently she 'couldn't find the information on Google'. I actually turned around in my seat and stared at her, which I know is a stuffy old 40-something thing to do, but I couldn't help it. All I could think was 'No child of mine will think googling is research!'.

Call me old-fashioned, but I think being able to use an index is a valid skill. I could be wrong, though. My mother wouldn't let me learn how to type because she was worried I would become a secretary like her. This turned out to be a poor decision as I still can't touch-type. I've written way more than a million words with a computer now and I still have to look at the keys.

They are the only kid with a bibliography attached to their grade 4 essay

I laughed when @MisaimedBrain asked me on Twitter: 'How old is Thesis Whisperer Jnr? I'm imagining a small child developing impeccable referencing.' It's funny because it's true. Part of the fight over the last piece of homework was my insistence on correct footnoting and formatting of the bibliography. Poor little bastard.

But there may be hope for Thesis Whisperer Jnr and me after all. The next day, on the way home, I asked him how his project on Ireland was going: 'Well, I still got to draw a leprechaun, because I wrote under it "Some people might believe in leprechauns". That's not a generalisation, is it, Mum?'

4

BEING A WRITER

In his superb book *Writing for Social Scientists* (which should be renamed *Writing for Everyone, Anywhere*), Howard Becker talks about the importance of being the kind of writer who can get stuff Out The Door. He suggests writers need to think more like companies who make gadgets like phones and computers. Corporations have to stick to shipping schedules if they want to stay in business. The engineers will want to delay shipping until the product matches the vision in their heads, but the marketing people will be happy with 'good enough'. Even if the new gadget is rough around the edges, the marketing people will still make the engineers get it Out The Door. According to Becker, the logic of the marketing people is simple: if it sells, there will be money to build the next version. The next version will be better, but, meanwhile, this one will do.

I have reluctantly come to the conclusion that one must take a pragmatic attitude to writing in academia, or you will quickly drown. We can rail against the quality and quantity metrics which dominate academia – and I do, all the time – but they are a fact of life for now. In my opinion, it's only going to become increasingly competitive and the pressure to write more will not ease up any time soon, so we need to find ways to mobilise our writing energy as best we can. As Becker points out: people will judge you on what you have done, not the ideas you have in your head.

In this collection of posts I have left out my most popular posts on writing, which describe in detail various aspects of writing technique. One of my most popular posts ever is How to Write 1000 Words a Day. After running the Thesis Boot Camp program at ANU for a number of years, I upgraded my estimates of a possible daily output to 10 000 words a day. How to Write 10 000 Words a Day and Not Go Batshit Crazy is my definitive guide to busting out words on deadline. I follow up with Why You Might Be 'Stuck', as it speaks to some of the more difficult-to-diagnose writer's block moments.

Blog posts on writing technique are helpful, but there are deeper issues underlying most writing problems. Writing 'headspace' and process issues are the subject of this group of posts. In The Academic Writers' Strike I set the scene by describing some of the dubious business practices of corporate academic journal publishers and the effects they have on our ability to continue to make knowledge. Every time we publish, we are committing a political act. Blogging offers a quick and easy way to bring knowledge out from behind the paywalls of academic journals. It is one way to resist the perverse effects of the 'metricisation' of academic work because no one has (yet) developed a productivity metric for it, such as the dreaded h-index.

Several posts in this group tackle the topic of reading. By the time you get to the PhD, you might know how to read academic jargon in your field, but you don't necessarily know how to read at scale, nor are you likely to have been given good strategies for finding literature and keeping track of your reading. Reading takes concentrated attention, which can be difficult to achieve amidst the constant demands of a teaching and research schedule.

Finally, that most unrewarding of writing tasks – email! It might seem weird to include a post about such a mundane form of writing, but email is a theme I have returned to repeatedly on the blog – mostly because I see it as one of the main killers of writing productivity. Email, She Wrote contains my best advice, honed over years, on managing email. It was great to revisit earlier posts on email while creating this one, to see how I was nudging towards a solution. I believe I have found one, for myself at least, which I share with you in the hope it will help you face the daily electronic deluge with good cheer.

Collectively, these posts might help you recognise when your inner engineering department does not have your best interests at heart. Listen to your marketing department instead, and repeat after me: 'Perfect is the enemy of Done.' Speaking of which – I'm off to finish editing the rest of this book. My internal marketing department is telling me: 'Just ship it!'

THE ACADEMIC WRITERS' STRIKE

I have spent years exhorting PhD students to publish as much as possible on the grounds you need to be published to have a chance at getting that first academic job. But I can't keep handing out this advice with a clear conscience. Academic publishing is presented as a universal good, without regard to how the publishing system operates. While publications are an essential addition to the CV in today's competitive job market, big publishers are using this to make boatloads of money – in the order of millions of dollars – from the labour we academics willingly give them for free. This profit largely goes into the pockets of shareholders, not the researchers or universities.

Essentially, this is public money which becomes 'privatised'. It works a bit like this. Australian citizens are taxed and the government uses this money to fund my university. My university pays me a wage to write papers, among other things. I give my papers, and the copyright to reproduce and distribute them, to an academic publisher. They publish my article in a big database and make it searchable. Then my university is forced to buy it back. It gets worse. We are taught that being a good academic citizen means doing peer reviews for these journals, thus helping to ensure the quality of the publishing system as a whole. And it gets worse still. Some journal publishers engage in questionable practices regarding how they sell the content we produce back to us. You may have heard of the term 'bundling'. Basically bundling works a bit like a cable television subscription. I like to watch the LifeStyle channel, but Thesis Whisperer Jnr likes the Discovery channel. My cable company is well aware of this but only sells 'bundles', not individual channels. I would like to buy just the LifeStyle and Discovery channels, but instead I am forced to buy two bundles, with a whole lot of crap I don't want to watch, in order to get both the channels we want. In this way, the TV company makes me pay more – increasing 'shareholder value' (which is just a way of saying making rich people even richer).

This system is making the cost of scholarship

unsustainable. Libraries have been facing increasing costs because of these bundling practices, and the problem is worse in the developing world. I have had emails from people in Africa and some parts of Asia asking for a copy of an article because their universities have had to cut costs. According to my publishing agreement I would be breaking the law to send it to them. You can probably guess what I do – but I won't admit to anything publicly for fear of being prosecuted.

Unfortunately, the academic publishing system is built into the university's DNA. To maintain our veneer of being a meritocracy, the university needs publishers to help them weigh up the merits of each of its researchers. If I publish in good-quality journals, they have a way of judging my quality as an academic. If I completely refuse to participate, I will not get promoted and I may even lose my job. Journal publishers use this as just one among a range of specious arguments for how they provide 'value' to academics. Maintaining large database systems and editing our papers is not cost-free – true. Everyone has the right, I believe, to be paid for his or her work, but the argument can easily run the other way. Journal publishers pay their shareholders, their editors, administrators and software engineers – so where's my cut as content provider and expert consultant?

Some academics have become so incensed at what they see as the inequities of this system that they have signed the Cost of Knowledge petition (<www.the-costofknowledge.com>), declaring they will boycott the journal publisher Elsevier. Elsevier are not the only journal to be accused of questionable practices, but they have copped the brunt of the academic anger. This petition is the academic equivalent of the Hollywood writers' strike. I think it could work, so, after some hesitation, I signed it. It's not, of course, the whole answer. It only targets one publisher, but it's the only way I can send a message loud enough to be heard.

I have to be honest with you, though: I only signed because the effect on me personally is slight. Elsevier publishes very few education journals. Would I have signed a similar petition against Taylor & Francis? I'm not sure. Those of us earlier in our careers have much more to lose, being political. Journal publishers seem blissfully unaware of the challenge to their business model posed by social media and easy, free publishing tools. If I wanted to, I could start my own peer-reviewed journal tomorrow. I have the tools and the contacts, just not the time … Recently, in a public forum, I challenged a member of the Elsevier board to tell me how the company is responding to changes in the publishing landscape. He told me they are thinking about it, and in the meantime they were generously providing, free of charge, a guide to publishing in journals for first-timers. The first hit is always free, right?

I think we academics need to start learning from other creatives, like the music industry. Most pop stars get paid ludicrously small amounts for their creative work, but they do get paid something. We don't have to throw the baby out with the bathwater, but we could pressure the publishers to kick back some of that profit to the people who make research happen and advance human knowledge: us. I have no objection to journals making some money and providing work for editors and other talented people. So, Elsevier, I will start publishing with you when you start sharing the love. I have some ideas for how you can do it.

Let's start with simple profit-sharing. For instance, you could pay my institution a nominal amount per download. Perfect capitalist solution: the more popular my papers get, the more my institution benefits and they can reward me with a promotion. Or you could pay me directly for each download of my work and I could use that money to buy out teaching time and buy in research assistants. If you don't want to pay me or my institution, you could show me that you are a good corporate citizen in other ways. How about giving me some share options, or 'angel investing' in cutting-edge research? You could even benefit by getting a cut of the profits from our inventions. Or you could think about providing some grant money from your profits which content providers like myself could bid for on a competitive basis. Elsevier, you could actually *benefit* by being generous – if you play this right, you could get the first pick of all the best work because I would have an incentive to choose you. (I am available as a consultant if you need more ideas for increasing 'shareholder value' at your next board meeting – for a small fee, of course.)

At the time of writing, the Cost of Knowledge petition had 16 489 signatures – and it's growing continuously. The pressure is starting to mount from institutions too. Many have announced open access policies, but this has just resulted in the corporate journal publishers upping the fees to make things open access. Slapping on another charge is not the answer and is only going to make those of us who get the implications of this rent-seeking behaviour more pissed off. Recently, a group of major universities in Germany announced they would no longer purchase Elsevier journals. I've watched this situation for years and still the corporate journal publishers continue to pursue these outdated and harmful business models. What will it take to make changes happen?

Part of the problem is that early-career researchers or students do not feel they are in a position to sign on to the boycott. I'm not judging. Whatever gets you through the night. I do, however, applaud the senior members of our community who are providing leadership and showing the way. If enough of you with little to lose sign the petition, those of us at the bottom of the academic pecking order might feel more confident to pile on. It's my hope that corporate journal publishers will be forced to be more generous and creative – or die. It's urgent that we fix these problems. Corporate publishers can provide an excellent service for academia – if their business models are revised. It's urgent the sector does this work because I'm not sure we academics have the resources to replace the work they do.

 IN PRAISE OF ACADEMIC JARGON

I like coffee.

I mean – I REALLY like coffee. I don't smoke anymore and rarely drink. Caffeine is the only vice I have left. People tell me all the time that it's unhealthy, but as far as I'm concerned you can tear the coffee from my cold dead hands.

I grew up in a lower middle-class family of committed tea drinkers. 'Coffee' meant a powdered concoction called International Roast which might be, at least in part, the sweepings from the coffee house floor. If you got the temperature of the water just right, you would sometimes get a slight froth on the surface. I later learned that this froth was meant to mimic the 'crema' at the top of an espresso. I'm not sure what chemical means were used to achieve this faux crema, but I suspect it had something to do with detergent. When my family wanted to impress a guest they would roll out the Moccona. This came in a fancy jar and was not a powder, but actual granules. There were glossy ads on TV for Moccona, so my mother thought it was Classy. It tasted marginally better than poor old International Roast and until I went to university it was my gold standard in the coffee department.

My middle-class university friends introduced me to what we in Australia call a 'coffee plunger' (what everyone else in the world calls a 'French press', for reasons unknown). Plunger coffee was a revelation: almost as easy to make as instant coffee and much less likely to cause stomach aches. I abandoned instant coffee and never looked back. Plunger coffee was just better and allowed more scope for experimentation. I learned that the plunger coffee could be improved by keeping the ground coffee in the fridge or, better still, by buying beans whole and grinding them myself.

I went to university in the 1990s and in that decade the food culture in the city of Melbourne blossomed. Waves of migrants brought their coffee with them. I happily explored this strange new caffeinated world. My coffee repertoire expanded further: strong Turkish coffee, Vietnamese coffee with condensed milk, tiny aromatic egg cups of spiced Saudi Arabian brew and, of course, the Italian espresso. Each and every one has a special place in my heart.

Coffee has been an education. I've learned special words to use when ordering coffee. These 'coffee jargon' words are useful if you want your coffee to taste exactly the way you like it. For example, I usually don't want a strong coffee in the afternoon. At the cafe I used to say 'Can I have a half-strength shot topped up with water and a splash of skim milk?' and then spend the next couple of minutes answering questions from the barista – how much water? How much milk? Perhaps just a full shot in a bigger cup? Now I just order a ristretto, which is the first, sweetest bit of the coffee topped up with milk. With each bit of coffee jargon under my belt, life got just a little bit simpler.

By now you are probably wondering why I am banging on about coffee, but bear with me because there are similarities between coffee jargon and academic jargon. Both involve insider language which takes specialised knowledge, time and experience to understand. Just as using coffee jargon can make you sound like a coffee snob at your old tea-drinking grandmother's house, academic jargon is all about the context. It's scary easy to overdo it and look like a novice just pretending to understand the academic grown-ups. There's no doubt that academic jargon makes text harder to read and will limit your audience. Some argue that using academic jargon is a way of reinforcing class boundaries and creating an unhealthy distance from 'ordinary people'. But we need this academic jargon because it makes our texts simultaneously concise and dense with meaning.

For instance, I could say this:

Academic jargon is created when we talk to each other about difficult topics and want to create a shared understanding using fewer words. We therefore create shorter words as 'placeholders'. Over time, with use, these words become more commonly known and their meaning becomes more 'stable'. For example, academic teachers share them with students. Books use the terms and spread them from person to person and across national boundaries. The words are used in speech in special places – like classrooms – where people can seek and get clarification on the developing collective meaning of the terms. Gradually, incrementally, the circle of people who understand and can use the shared terms grows.

Or I could merely say this:

Academic jargon is insider language created through a range of discursive practices among specialists.

See? Much easier! If you know what discursive practices are, of course.

Each piece of academic jargon is actually a complex bundle of ideas from which the knowledgeable reader can unpack the relevant bit of meaning in relation to the rest of the sentence. To complicate matters, academic disciplines do jargon in different ways. If you pay close attention, you will see how the way we do jargon connects with the way we do knowledge. Scientists have short names for processes and compounds and formulas which express the way parts of the natural world relate to each other. Artists use ordinary words like 'organic', 'texture' and 'tone', but in their hands these words change their meaning and become poetic, if in a slightly slippery way. Business academics have lots of compound terms that stick ideas together and make new ones, like 'behavioural economics'.

Academics need to make new kinds of jargon all the time or our texts would be extraordinarily long and more ambiguous than they need to be. We'd be constantly asking each other the academic equivalent of 'How much water? and 'How much milk?'. This can make academic texts hard to translate into plain language. Translation always involves a shift in meaning. A ristretto is not a half shot topped up with water and a splash of milk – it's a completely different drink. Recently, on her blog, scholar and academic writing expert Pat Thomson pointed out that talking to the ordinary person through 'engaging with the media' is not as simple a task as it sounds. She's so right. Unpacking academic jargon and explaining the ideas in 'plain language that anyone can understand' is extremely laborious, even dangerously reductive. As much as I'm a fan of the three-minute thesis, an international competition where PhD students compete to give the best short verbal presentation, helping students make these scripts is a painful process as they are acutely aware of how much meaning gets lost.

Academic jargon is wonderful, but, like good coffee, it is an acquired taste. Sometimes plain language is good enough to get the heart started. I travel a lot, as you will know if you follow me on Instagram. Occasionally I encounter International Roast in the coffee rooms of academia and I always greet it like an old friend. My academic host will invariably apologise for not having a 'proper' coffee machine, but I don't mind. It's unpretentious stuff which brings back childhood memories and I'm more or less immune to its chemical charms. Given the choice, though, I will always drink a 'real coffee' when I'm at home because – well, it's just better.

SURVIVING THE READING MARATHON

In grade 4 I had to find out the name of the Japanese prime minister for a school assignment. I went to my version of Google at the time – my parents – but they didn't know. They tried to help me find the information at the local library, using the back issues of newspapers. When that failed we asked neighbours and relatives – true story. No one knew. Finally my mother had the bright idea of ringing the Japanese Embassy, who bemusedly supplied the information.

In 1979 there was no ready source of real-time political information other than the mass media. If the newspaper or TV didn't do a story about the Japanese prime minister that week, you were hosed. Nowadays, of course, I could find that information in less than a second – even if I am wandering in a park somewhere – thanks to my trusty phone (or, as a PhD student called it once, 'the tiny box of all knowing'). This ready availability of information is both a boon and a curse to scholars. There's just so much 'stuff' out there which relates to almost every topic that it's literally impossible to process it all.

The feeling of being overwhelmed by information starts in the PhD and doesn't get any easier as you move on in your career. I often meet students who are stuck in some kind of reading death spiral, crushed under the weight of all this information. Most often, this problem manifests as slow writing, but sometimes the problem is so bad that people become paralysed by doubt and can't write at all. Their dilemma is totally understandable. Not only do you have to absorb a lot of information, you are being force-fed opinions while trying to develop your own. Doing a literature review is a bit like going to a party where you don't know anyone. It can be tempting to just stand in the corner, awkwardly holding your drink. It takes courage to find your voice in the noise of other people's thoughts – which is what research writing is. The overwhelming temptation is to wait until you have 'read enough' before you risk putting your oar in. The problem is, if you are doing research in the right way, you never will.

Developing different reading methods can help. You have to learn to read like a 'mongrel', as my friend John Ting says. For those who are not up with Australian slang, a mongrel is a dog of uncertain parentage who is usually ugly, but who survives by being cunning and tough. Reading like a mongrel means you forget about chapter order, reading the introduction or checklists to help you do proper 'critical reading'. You scan the text rapidly, use indexes, the search function, Google Books or whatever; you go straight for the bit that you absolutely have to know and leave the rest for later. It isn't pretty, but it works. The key to reading like a mongrel is knowing what it is you need to find out. My nine-year-old self had a singular focus: find out the name of the Japanese prime minister. With academic work it's easy to lose focus and explore the side paths because there are so many bits of information you need to assemble. A certain amount of wandering aimlessly through the online journal catalogue is productive, but too much will leave you lost in the wilderness.

The reading problem is one you will deal with all through a PhD and beyond. Reading effectively and efficiently is a learnable skill which is not often explicitly taught – but it should be. You see, it's a reading marathon you are on, my friends. A marathon has its own kind of grim fun, I'm sure, but it's mostly exhausting. You need to be well prepared to run a marathon, or you might die. Here are three ideas to help you prepare for and survive the reading marathon, which I share in my note-taking workshops.

Remember: it's a capsule collection, not a jumble sale

I have a weakness for those TV reality shows like *Mary Queen of Shops*, and *What Not to Wear*, where fashion experts help clueless punters build 'capsule collections' by making them sort through mountains of unflattering clothes (with many tears in the process). Academic reading, especially for a thesis, is a similar problem. Ultimately your thesis should contain a carefully-thought-out selection of the mass of literature you have read. I'm reliably informed by friends in the fashion biz that the way to compose a capsule collection is to choose a base colour that goes with everything and two accent colours. In literature terms, this translates as finding the key authors and/or research groups that produce stuff that is most closely aligned to your work and then reading 'outwards', using the bibliographies on these papers as your guide.

Identifying these key players is easier if you perform strategic citation searches. A citation search is a good indication of popularity, but not always quality. However, popular papers are a good place to start seeing what everyone is talking about. A good tool for analysing citations is Publish or Perish, designed and built by the University of Melbourne scholar Anne-Wil Harzing. Publish or Perish uses Google Scholar to perform the analysis (note: if you are on a Mac like me you will need to have some kind of Windows emulator). If that sounds too complicated, you can perform a citation search in most scholarly databases. Visit your library to find out the tricks; time well spent, I assure you.

Ditch the paper

Look, I get that paper is a nice format to read. Portable and easy to mark up. I agree that there is nothing quite as satisfying as scribbling 'WHAT??!!' and 'WRONG!!' in the margins of a paper you dislike, but people – it's time to face facts: an obsession for paper will hold you back as a scholar. Reading electronically allows you to read like a proper mongrel. A simple word search is the best tool for finding the 'meaty' parts of a paper or a book, without getting too invested in it. Try searching for 'signpost' language such as: 'This paper argues that', 'In this paper we explore' or 'The main question is' – or better still, just the words 'argue', 'explore' or 'question'. Look for certain verbs as well, for example 'shown', 'proven', 'suggest', 'question', 'query' and 'challenge'. Another trick is to look for words that modify arguments such as 'may', 'might', 'possibly', and so on. Certain words will be important to your work, so keep a ledger of the ones that appear in papers that you find useful.

Time yourself

Editing a multi-authored book is a nightmare because so few academics meet the deadline. Most academics I know work extremely hard, so this inability to meet a deadline is an enduring mystery. I suspect that all that hard work is not as efficient as it could be. I certainly see plenty of inefficient habits get passed on to PhD students. Maybe it's my architecture background, but I think a deadline is a deadline. Meeting a deadline means knowing how long it takes you to do something. I emphasised the 'you' in that sentence because people work at different speeds depending on experience, time of day and level of stress, among other things. I'm not putting myself forward as a super-efficient academic worker (one of my staff used to describe my job as 'having coffee with people'), but I do measure myself so I can gauge how long it will take me to do something.

It's important to do this measuring periodically and systematically to make sure you can make accurate projections. For example, I know that a 1000-word blog post takes me, on average, two hours (when I first started they used to take four hours). It will take me up to a day to produce a page of academic text, but it depends on what I am writing. Writing data, where I have largely done the thinking work, takes less time than writing literature reviews, introductions or conclusions. And tools matter a great deal to writing speed. My sister, Anitra, measured herself and noticed she was four times faster in Scrivener than in MS Word.

I have just timed my reading and I have improved a lot since I last measured myself, two years ago. It takes me around 20 minutes to read an academic paper in my field, which is about 1 minute and 40 seconds per page (I highlighted some stuff to come back to, but didn't take notes). It will take me over two and a half minutes per page with academic text that's difficult or unfamiliar to me (again with highlighting, not writing notes). I only take notes when I have to write a paper, but I know that note taking will double, at least, the time I spend reading a paper. Once you know your speed you can estimate how many papers you can realistically read in the time you have available.

CURING READITIS

2015 was a busy year, both personally and professionally. I raised a glass on New Year's Eve with a sense of multiple jobs well done and dusted. Family Thesis Whisperer renovated a house and moved into it, putting down proper Canberra roots. I lost my 'baby weight' (Thesis Whisperer Jnr is now taller than me, so it was way past time) and started running. The blog went from strength to strength and a significant research project got off the ground. With a fantastic team at ANU, I ran the massive open online course called 'How to Survive Your PhD' with over 13 000 enrolments, and over 800 people attended the ANU Three Minute Thesis competition.

Oh, and I got promoted to associate professor.

One of the small, but significant, achievements for me in 2015 was becoming a much more tidy person at home and at work. For years Mr Thesis Whisperer has complained about picking up after me, but ever since my friend Megan McPherson recommended Marie Kondo's bestselling *The Life-Changing Magic of Tidying Up* he's had no need to complain. Megan was way ahead of the hype curve on the Marie Kondo tidying craze. I had never heard of the Japanese clutter-busting guru when she enthused about it, but it was cheap in Kindle and I trust Megan's taste, so I bought it.

I read *The Life-Changing Magic of Tidying Up* greedily, in one sitting, like it was a box of chocolates. If you are put off by the hype, don't be. It's a fun and engaging book, part self-help and memoir, part philosophy, and a light read for those of us accustomed to dense texts full of academic jargon. The so-called KonMari method is disarmingly simple: only keep possessions which bring you joy and are useful – ideally both. I started KonMari-ing with clothes, sorting first by category. I took every top out of my closet and held each one up in turn, asking myself 'Does this top bring me joy?' To my surprise, I got rid of most of them. I then moved on to the kitchen and reduced my collection of tools and cutlery by at least half. KonMari-ing is a surprisingly intense process that, of course, only the truly privileged will ever experience. I was forced to face my conspicuous consumption, and it wasn't pretty. Luckily, Canberra has the fantastic Green Shed initiative, so I was able to donate to others, rather than landfill.

I ended up keeping only about a quarter of my wardrobe. Less choice about what to wear meant less time getting ready and far more time drinking coffee and reading the Interwebs. I was hooked and started discarding with gay abandon. Most of my jewellery box, knick-knacks and books were soon gone. Mr Thesis Whisperer was so impressed with the results he joined in the Great Kitchen Purge of 2015. Part of the KonMari method is to have a designated place for everything you keep, so we had long, intense discussions about kitchen scales and serving platters. Gradually the pantry and fridge were transformed from crowded places where sauce bottles go to die to efficient, clean storage zones.

Friends started remarking on how scary tidy our place had become.

Unlike other life changes I have attempted, the KonMari way seemed to stick. I started carefully considering new purchases by measuring them against my personal 'joy index'. As a consequence, I bought less and started treating what I have with much more care and respect. As promised by Ms Kondo, tidying now feels like a natural process, not a chore. I actually enjoy folding all my stockings and socks into my drawers.

I started to wonder – might the KonMari method work to bring a sense of peace, control and order to my work life too? I am very 'other motivated' in my work. The various reports and deliverables that go with my role as Director of Research Training are done well in advance because other people are expecting them. My teaching is very organised thanks to proper training and business processes I have honed carefully over the years. My blog schedule is sorted out a year in advance because my valued readers expect to see something weekly and I don't want to disappoint them.

But my research work? Always in a shambles.

Unlike the rest of my work duties, my research schedule is largely set by me, and is therefore a mess. I get research outputs done, but I rely on others for motivation. As a consequence, I haven't published a solo-authored paper since 2011. Unless I am collaborating or writing a book for a publishing deadline, I will always find something else to do with my time. The reading problem is even worse than the writing problem. Reading is just not a priority, but it is a source of constant anxiety. I never do enough, or properly digest what I do read. One of my students, Jodie, calls this feeling of constantly being in a reading deficit 'Readitis': a disorder bought on by the vast amount of literature available and the limited time in which to absorb it.

I've started to think about how KonMari methods

might be applied to this Readitis problem. My first step was to pick a soft target. Like many academics, I download far more papers than I will ever read. My 'research closet' had ballooned out to over 2000 references, mostly filed in Papers3. In late November, I spent a couple of hours every evening opening the papers, thinking about why I had each one and how it fitted into my various research interests. Unless there was a clear reason to keep a paper, it was deleted. In the first pass I discarded all but two of the 600 or so papers I had collected for my PhD. Those papers had clearly served their purpose, but I still had around 1000 papers left – more than I would ever read or need, especially as I usually do a comprehensive literature search before starting a new project anyway.

The problem of these remaining references was, I realised, similar to the problem of KonMari-ing my underwear. I had plenty of good, serviceable underwear and the temptation was to keep it all, but it was taking up a lot of space. So I bought baskets that fitted into my drawers sized to hold two week's supply – the longest possible time between washing loads. Then I simply put the best underwear in the baskets and threw the rest out. Similarly, I started reducing my papers by creating 'playlists' of themes. I ended up with hundreds and hundreds of papers which didn't fit clearly into any of these collections. It caused me a bit of a pang to press delete on these, but I did it. Now I had only 681 papers in my database, which has crept up to 754 in the year since I purged. This is still more than half a million words – presumably more than I need – but I'm feeling more in control.

Purging and organising is not a cure for Readitis – perhaps more in the nature of a treatment that helps manage the condition. My collections set useful boundaries and help me start on the reading with a sense of purpose.

This process of discarding research material might not be for everyone. I tweeted about it and many academics expressed horror at the prospect of throwing so many papers into the virtual bonfire. Other people told me they are applying the KonMari 'less is more' philosophy to data or to notes – even to supervisors! Who knows, the clutter-free academic life might bring joy after all.

💬 WORMHOLE LITERATURE

I have a friend, let's call her Jenny. Jenny is about six months into her research degree and just beginning to discover the true extent of the literature which might be relevant to her topic, by which I mean she's completely freaking out.

Initially, Jenny enjoyed the process. She read things her supervisor suggested and then went off exploring, using the references in those papers as a starting point. Her subject librarian taught her about databases and how to use Google Scholar properly (not everything is in there, just so you know). The librarian also taught her how keywords work and how to do citation searches. With these new mad skills of library Jenny discovered a vast amount of stuff, which, although it was interesting, seemed only peripherally related to her topic.

Jenny did everything right. She discussed ideas she had read about with her supervisors and some of her peers. She wrote a bit, then read some more. Under the influence of the literature, her ideas about her thesis changed. The same names started appearing, which helped Jenny understand how various scholars were linked together in skeins of thought. Being a social type of person, Jenny did a bit of academic networking and started to know some of the people who wrote those papers. This made her feel more confident. Comfortable even. Part of a community. That is, until she downloaded THAT PAPER.

Jenny didn't realise how important THAT PAPER was at first. She downloaded it as part of a conference proceeding, read it and tucked it away in her database as 'interesting, but not relevant'. There it might have stayed, unloved, had she not had her paper proposal accepted at the next iteration of that conference. This prompted Jenny to dig out the proceedings again to get a feel for the length and tone of the papers. Suddenly THAT PAPER spoke to her. On the second read, it seemed to touch on every idea that she had thought about so far, but – you know – in a better way. THAT PAPER took her half-formed ideas and wrapped beautiful words around them. Although it didn't precisely scoop her thesis topic, THAT PAPER showed her that she had only been reading in the shallow end of the pool. The reference list was full of papers Jenny had not read. This was a surprise. She read some of the referenced papers and, as it turns out, all of them were interesting, relevant – even important. Jenny started to see THAT PAPER as a godsend. It was, if you like, a set of goggles that enabled her to swim in the deep end of the pool.

Then an uncomfortable thought intruded: what might have happened if she had not bothered to read that paper twice? What if she had carried on, without knowing that all this other literature existed? What might her examiners, who surely would have read all those papers, have thought of her? They would think she was a bad scholar! She was going to fail! Cue a panicked phone call to me (I get a lot of calls like this – I'm a useful friend to have when you are doing a PhD). I tried to tell Jenny that she was borrowing trouble. She had now read THAT PAPER. All those terrible things wouldn't happen. My calming words had little effect; she was far from reassured. Why, she asked me, was the utter importance of THAT PAPER not clear the first time she read it? How had she missed all this other literature it pointed to?

Clearly Jenny's new, mad skills of library were deeply shaken, so I promised this post. You see, the feelings Jenny was experiencing are completely normal. In fact, realising you have just missed a piece of important literature is number four in the Thesis Whisperer's top five #phdemotions. In case you were wondering, here is the complete list:

1   Elation when you realise you know more than your supervisor about your topic and you feel brave enough to argue about it.
2   Fear of being 'found out' as fraud, not really knowing enough/being smart enough to be PhD student.
3   Unexpected admiration of your own writing.

4   The 'I'm a genius! Why hasn't anybody thought to
     do that before?' moment before people point out
     the obscure paper you've not read.
5   Misplaced smugness after photocopying/down-
     loading loads of stuff but not actually reading it.

Let's tackle each of these dilemmas in turn.

Question:
Why didn't Jenny see how important
THAT PAPER was the first time she read it?

Answer:
Sometimes you can't see the gorillas.

There's a difference, artists have long argued, between
looking and seeing. Looking involves taking in a scene
with your eyes; seeing involves making meaning from
it. The key to making meaning is salience: recognising
something as important and worth noticing. It's surprisingly easy to miss the relevance of other people's work,
partly, perhaps, because of how we are wired to look at
new stuff in the first place.

There's a famous experiment that is a good demonstration of the difference between seeing and looking.
When participants were asked to watch a video and

count the number of passes basketball players were making, most completely failed to notice a guy wearing a gorilla suit wandering through the scene, even when he stopped to beat his chest. When you watch the video knowing the gorilla is there it is almost impossible to believe that people could miss him – but remember, those people were primed to look for a ball being passed, not for gorillas. Since they were not primed to look for a gorilla, they literally did not see it.

I suspect this is what happened to Jenny on the first reading of THAT PAPER. She hadn't yet read enough to know what she should be looking for. She wasn't yet primed to see the meaning. Just as you can't understand a whole conversation from two lines of dialogue, academic papers rarely make sense in isolation. Re-reading is an important part of the reading process. If you don't see the point the first, second or even third read, you have not made a mistake – you just haven't seen the gorilla yet. Or there may be no gorillas to be seen. Getting to know literature is like watching a picture come into focus. Be patient, just keep reading.

Question:
What would have happened if Jenny had not re-found this paper 'by accident'?

Answer:
There are no accidents.

The first thing Jenny needs to realise is that she didn't rediscover this paper by accident at all. I contend that even if Jenny hadn't gone looking for those conference proceedings for another reason, she still would have rediscovered the paper, probably via a citation. I routinely download articles without realising I already have them until my database tells me. I'm experienced enough to realise this is not because I have made an error; it just happens. I can't possibly keep everything I have ever read in my head. I read at least 2000 words a day – maybe more; this is nearly three quarters of a million words a year. Over the three years you write your PhD you can expect to read at least 2 000 000 words. It's hardly surprising you don't remember everything. Procedures are important for this exact reason. So long as Jenny kept on doing exactly what she was doing – reading, writing, thinking, talking – she would eventually have found, if not everything, enough of it to convince the examiners that she is a competent scholar.

Question:
How had Jenny 'missed' all that other literature?

Answer:
THAT PAPER was a piece of wormhole literature.

One of my favourite TV shows is *Stargate SG-1*, mostly because of the way Samantha Carter kicks ass, but also because of the wormhole itself. It's a fantastic magic device that catapults our heroes to another world, in seconds. The distance between planets is so vast the show would be pretty boring without it. Just like the galaxy, the distance between researchers can sometimes be vast. Sometimes, even travelling at light speed, it can take a long time to get somewhere. As more and more knowledge is added to the pile, the connections between them become paper thin. Since we have to navigate literature mostly by connections, we can sometimes miss whole regions of the research universe. THAT PAPER was a research wormhole; it catapulted Jenny into a whole new area of potentially relevant literature. Again I say, if Jenny had just kept doing what she was doing, she would have found most if not all of those papers eventually. THAT PAPER merely helped Jenny, briefly, bend the laws of research physics for a moment – and that's got to be a good thing.

A JOURNAL ARTICLE BY ANY OTHER NAME

One of my most popular workshops is 'Write that Journal Article in Seven Days'. I've delivered this workshop nearly 80 times in the last six years with a slide share deck which has now had over 110 000 views. I'm so practised at this workshop that I can walk in and deliver it with no preparation, which is a good thing for a busy person. It took about 20 goes to get the slide deck right and then it stayed as it was for years and years.

Some of the slides have always worked better than others and (to be honest) it needed a refresh for a few years, but, like I said – busy. Recently, however, I ran a Thesis Boot Camp with a group of students who were unusually happy. Instead of doing academic advising I spent a lot of time noodling around my office, rearranging my books, doing the filing and digging into my long-term to-do list. I'm glad I did get around to working on this particular slide deck, because I was able to add a lot more stuff on article titles. You see, the title of your paper (or chapter, for that matter) can be a really good place to do some high-level thinking. A good title can help you decide the direction you want to take and the data you need to collect.

I got this idea from the book *Mapping Your Thesis*

by Dr Barry White. White claims there are only certain kinds of paper title: questions, explorations, statements, investigations, hypotheses and thesis. Writing the title first is a way of working backwards from a desired outcome in order to decide what kind of data you might want to collect and what kind of analyses might be appropriate. Let's say that my teenaged son, Thesis Whisperer Jnr, wants to write a paper to convince me to let him play more computer games. He could try the simplest strategy, writing the paper title as a *question*, like so: 'Is Kerbal Space Program more educational than Team Fortress?'. This title implies that the paper will be measuring and comparing the relative merits of one program against another. This paper might convince me of which program is a better use of his time, but not whether or not he should spend more time gaming. He could, instead, pose the paper title as an *investigation*: 'The online gaming platform Steam: which games are kids are playing most?'. This paper might give me some background information on what other parents allow their kids to play, but since I've never really cared what other parents do, it's unlikely to earn him more game time.

If Thesis Whisperer Jnr writes the title as an *exploration* of the topic of gaming it might be more persuasive. He could try a title like: 'The educational outcomes of kids who game a lot'. He would then have to define 'educational outcomes', perhaps by means of an indicator like grade point average. He could test this idea further by writing a paper with a *hypothesis* as a title: 'If kids game, they will get better grades'. I'd imagine this would be some kind of controlled study where he measured the outcomes of one group of kids who gamed with those of another group who didn't. I'd be into this – I do like a bit of data to inform my parenting decisions. If the results of these two papers showed there was a measurable effect of gaming on grades, he could follow up with another paper title posed as a *statement*, something like 'Kids and gaming: the benefits for parents', drawing on data generated in the two previous papers to make the case.

Better still, he could write all these papers and collect the evidence in a paper with a *thesis*-style title (remember: the definition of a thesis is a position you are taking on an issue). This final paper could be something like 'Kids learn more from gaming than from their teachers'.

Did you see what I did there? I defined a whole thesis just through thinking of a series of titles. If Thesis Whisperer Jnr wrote all those, he could definitely have more gaming time. Actually, next time he complains about his gaming privileges I might just hand him this study design and say 'Do this first'.

Heh.

Anyway, I digress. Titles are becoming increasingly important as a way for scholars to navigate the literature and decide what to download. There is some evidence that Google Scholar has placed more emphasis on the title than the journal where the paper is located, making databases and journals less important than the paper's title and the text excerpt Google generates. Anything that undermines the corporate dominance of the academic journal publishers is a good thing in my book. There's some useful literature on the titles academics give their work, most of it written by James Hartley from Keele University. My favourite is his paper 'There's more to the title than meets the eye: exploring the possibilities', in which Hartley lays out 12 different types of title.

Let's use Thesis Whisperer Jnr as an example again. Here's how he could create Hartley's 12 types of paper title types:

- A title that announces the general subject: 'The effect of playing Kerbal Space Program on teenagers' grade point average'.
- A specific theme following a general heading (these papers usually have a semi-colon in them): 'Teenage gamers: the relation between hours spent gaming and grades at school'.
- A title which indicates a controlling question: 'Is gaming a waste of time for teenagers?'
- A title that indicates that an answer will be revealed: 'Playing computer games increases teenagers' grade point average'.

- A title that indicates the position the author will take: 'Gaming is good for teenagers' mental health and social development'.
- A title that indicates the methodology used: 'Teenage gaming: a survey of the literature'.
- A title that is suggestive of guidelines or comparisons (these have become popular titles in the blogging genre): '19 ways that playing computer games boost teenager grade point averages'.
- A title that bids for attention using a startling or unusual statement: '"It's educational, Mum!": an analysis of negotiations between teenage gamers and their carers'.
- A title that bids for attention using alliteration (the same letter at the start of most of the words): 'PvP, PvE and perpetually perplexed parents'.
- A title that bids for attention by using literary or biblical allusions: 'To raid or not to raid? An analysis of teenage gamer friendships'.
- A title that bids for attention through using a pun: 'I'll be your player 1 if you'll be my player 2: teenage gamers and dating'.
- Straight-out mystifying or confusing titles: 'Mum said Whiskey Foxtrot Tango'.

I hope I've convinced you that taking time to deeply consider the title of a piece of work is worthwhile.

Every paper you write is competing with many others for attention. No one really knows how many academic journal articles there are online, but some estimate there are more than 50 million and others estimate that the majority of academic papers are never cited. That's centuries of human effort, wasted.

HOW TO WRITE 10 000 WORDS A DAY AND NOT GO BATSHIT CRAZY

Some years ago now, I tweeted a link to an article called 'How to write 1000 words a day for your blog', which I thought had some good productivity tips for thesis writers. @webnemesis wrote back: 'would like to see someone write a blog post on how to write 1000 words of substance for yr dissertation every day'.

Challenge accepted!

Towards the end of my PhD, I added up the number of words I had to write and divided them by the number of days of study leave I had left. Then I freaked out and had a little lie down. According to my calculations, I had to write 60 000 words in three months. After a cup of tea (with maybe just a whiff of scotch in it), I contemplated this problem and made a PLAN, cobbled together from all the advice books on writing I used in my workshops with doctoral students. A case of eating my own cooking, if you will.

A five-step plan to increase your writing output

This plan worked for me and I share it with you here. The plan works best at the end of a research project, when you have absorbed a lot of information about your topic and have thought about it for a long time. The basic premise follows Howard Becker's words of wisdom: there is no such thing as writing, only rewriting. The plan acknowledges that half the struggle of a thesis is to get stuff out of your head and onto the page in order to start the rewriting process. I've adapted this basic technique into the famous ANU Thesis Boot Camp Program and helped hundreds of students produce the first draft of most of their thesis in a single weekend. (Yes – it's possible. More on that in a bit.)

Step 1: Spend less time at your desk

Now close that Facebook window and listen to Aunty Thesis Whisperer for a moment. The secret to writing at least 1000 words a day is to give yourself a limited time frame in which to do it.

What's that I hear you say? 'Are you a crazy lady?!'

Well, I have learned by bitter experience that just because Mrs Bottom is paying a trip to Chair Town it does not always follow that productive work is being done. If you give yourself the whole day to write, you will spend the whole day writing and, in the process, drive yourself batshit crazy. One of my old teachers once said, 'Doing a thesis is like mucking out a stable'. His point was that you have to tackle it one wheelbarrow load of shit at a time. If you stay in the stable too long, the stink will kill you.

So dedicate less than a quarter of the day to making some new text and then take a break and return later to clean it up. This sounds counterintuitive, but trust me – it works.

Step 2: Remember the two-hour rule

I think most people only have about two really good, creative writing hours in a day. Only two hours in which new 'substantive' ideas make their way onto the page. Most of us are in the best frame of mind for this after breakfast and before lunch – whatever time of the day that happens to be for you (no judgment on your sleeping habits here). Writing new stuff should be almost the first thing you do when you sit down at your desk. Personally, I find it hard to resist the siren call of the email, but if I am on deadline I do an emergency scan and 'surface clean', then close it until lunchtime.

Step 3: Start in the middle

I don't even attempt to write introductions, conclusions or important transitions first. As Howard Becker said in his excellent book *Writing for Social Scientists*: 'How can I introduce it if I haven't written it yet?' This attitude is echoed in one of my favourite books, *Helping Doctoral Students Write*, where Barbara Kamler and Pat Thomson recommend writing in 'chunks', not chapters. A chunk can be anything up to two pages long: the text between each subheading, if you like. No doubt you have some scrappy notes which you can transcribe into your file to act as a 'seed'. Once you have planted the seed, just start adding on words around and over it – this builds a chunk. Don't worry about where the chunk fits in yet – that's a rewriting problem.

Step 4: Write as fast as you can, not as well as you can

This advice also comes from Becker, who points out that thinking is part of the process of writing. The surest way to slow the process is to worry too much about whether your thinking is any good. So – and this is very important – give yourself permission to write badly. *Really* badly if necessary. 'Make a mess and clean it up later' is Becker's advice.

The best way to sharpen the process of thinking in writing is to write really fast. Thought moves swiftly. Your attempts to write 'well' will slow you down and you won't capture your thinking. People at Thesis Boot Camp resist my exhortations to write fast, claiming that fast writing lacks precision. But that's missing the point. This kind of writing is to generate ideas – the 'shitty first draft' as my friend Liam Connell puts it (quoting Anne Lamott in *Bird by Bird*) – not to produce the final text. Proper word selection is critical in academic writing, but do it as part of refining your words, not drafting them, or it will put the brakes on your thinking. If you can't think of a word immediately, use another/equivalent/filler word. Later, go back and find the right word.

Do this 'generative writing' in bursts – most people can only sustain it for ten or 15 minutes. Time yourself. At first you might only be able to do it for three minutes. Use the timer as a training aid and try to extend the length of time to around ten minutes at least. When you need a rest from the sprint, review and fiddle with the text. Resolve your word choices, move sentences around, repair paragraphs – whatever floats your boat. Then plant a new seed and do another burst. Do this over and over until your writing window is done. It's likely you will produce more than 1000 words in two hours – in fact, I do upwards of 3000 messy words when I write like this. It's gruelling and bad for your back and shoulders, which is why the two-hour time limit is important.

Step 5: Leave it to rest ... then rewrite

Because you are writing without judgment, most of the words you generate in step 4 will be crap. Carving off the excess crap during the editing process will reveal the 1000 words of beautiful substantive text you are after. But take a break before you attempt this or you won't have the necessary perspective. Have a coffee with a friend, walk the dog, watch some TV – whatever takes you away from your desk for a couple of hours. Then come back, maybe after dinner, and start sifting through, massaging and editing that shitty first draft into something delightful.

Be strategic about this editing; some parts will be easier than others. You might need to save some difficult editing for the morning when you have 'washed your brain' with some sleep. Do try to pull some 'finished' words together, even if it's only a paragraph. This gives you a sense of achievement, which is vitally important for morale.

———

In a nutshell, that's how I wrote 60 000 words in three months. When I present this method in seminars it invariably horrifies those people who like to write line by perfect line. I'm sympathetic to the reasons people like to write that way, but it seems to me that they suffer a lot more pain than perhaps they need to.

How about *10 000* words a day?

I thought my plan was gold standard until I read Rachel Aaron's post How I Went from Writing 2000 Words to 10 000 Words a Day* and did a double-take.

Can you really write 10 000 words a day? Well, Rachel says she can, with three conditions. You need to:

1   Know what you are going to write before you write it.
2   Set aside a protected time to write.
3   Feel enthusiastic about what you are writing.

I read the post with interest. Much of what Rachel did conformed with my plan, but I couldn't bring myself to really believe Rachel's productivity claims. To regularly

---

* On her blog *Pretentious Title*, 8 June 2011.

write 10 000 words a day: it's the dream, right? Imagine if you could reliably write 10 000 words a day, how long would it take to finish your thesis … A week? How about a journal paper – a day?

Impossible!

Or so I thought. I'm now a 10 000 words a day believer because I have been watching students write even more than this in a single day at the Thesis Boot Camps we run at ANU. The Thesis Boot Camp formula was developed by Liam Connell and Peta Freestone of the University of Melbourne. Thesis Boot Camp (and the veterans' days which follow) is a total program designed to help late-stage PhD students finish the first draft of their thesis. The Thesis Boot Camp concept is simple – put a whole lot of PhD students in a room for a whole weekend and set them the goal of writing 20 000 words each. Yes – you heard me right. At least one student has achieved this goal at the Boot Camps I have run. More importantly, many students write many more words than they thought they would. We achieve this by putting Rachel Aaron's advice into practice.

1   Know what you are going to write before you write it

At Boot Camp we teach our students a range of generative writing strategies, but before this we ask the student to spend at least a week making a 'thesis map' to bring to Boot Camp. The map is essentially a series of subheadings which the students use as prompts for composing new text, or re-using existing text.

Students, particularly those in the humanities and arts, tend to agonise over the thesis document's 'structure'. I think the anxiety stems from the idea that 'thesis structure' is some kind of perfect platonic form they need to discover. It's not. Thesis structure is made, not found. Thesis structure is strongly influenced by disciplinary precedent and the content of the thesis itself. A history PhD might follow a timeline from the past to the present; a science PhD might echo the order of the experiments that have been performed. These theses are relatively easy to wrangle on the whole, but many people are doing multidisciplinary PhDs, or their PhD is located in education or the creative arts, which do not have comfortable traditions. This means you'll have to make the structure up. Try the following 'snowflake' technique:

- Try to capture an overview of the thesis by completing the following sentences (from the work of Rowena Murray):
  1 This thesis contributes to knowledge by …
  2 This thesis is important because …
  3 The key research question is …
  4 The sub-questions are …

- Decide how long your thesis will be. Most universities have a maximum word count. Aim for your thesis to be at least two thirds of this total. Using the generative writing method means you are likely to write more, so give yourself some wiggle room.
- Make a document with chapter headings and assign word counts. Include an introduction of 2000 to 3000 words, followed by up to seven chapters of equal length and a conclusion of around 4000 to 5000 words.
- It's counterintuitive, but have a go at writing down ideas for your conclusion. My PhD supervisor, Scott Drake, used to say that a thesis is like a joke: if you know the punchline you can perform it better. Study these closely and ask yourself: have you got data, theories, evidence and arguments to support these conclusions? These concluding points, singularly or in combination, will form the 'key learnings' of the thesis – knowledge and ideas you want your readers to absorb. This will put you in a better position to write the introduction.
- Include at least one key learning in each chapter, maybe more. Under each chapter heading, note the key learnings in the form of a brief synopsis of up to 300 words. This synopsis is like a mini-abstract

that explains what the rest of the chapter will be about.

- Make a list of the material you will include in the chapter as dot points. Don't worry about the gaps and stuff you haven't written yet, just make a note of them. These should be short sentences that will act as subheadings between which you will do your generative writing.
- Now ask yourself: if, at the end of the chapter, I want the reader to be convinced of the validity of this key learning, what needs to appear first? What comes next? And so on. Rearrange or write new subheadings as you go until you have arranged all the subheadings of the chapter in a way that tells the research story.

The technique I describe above is called a snowflake because it's a way of creating a skeleton to guide your writing that has enough flexibility to let ideas appear. Following these steps will help you to create the thesis map – but it's important to remember that this is merely an aid to writing, not a plan set in stone. You can change, add and move stuff around as you write.

In our Thesis Boot Camps we ask students to just pick a spot on this map and start writing as fast as they can, not as well as they can. Does this generate perfect thesis-ready text? Not necessarily, but many students say that the writing they produce at Boot Camp is clearer than the writing they did before it, when they were worrying over every word. I think the thesis map is a big part of this clarity because it keeps the focus tight.

This organising technique works best for very late-stage thesis students, but it can be a way of creating order and working out what you need to find out or write more about at any time in your journey.

2 Set aside a protected time to write

I've written heaps about this, so I won't rehash it all here. Just do it, OK?

3 Feel enthusiastic about what you are writing

I think this is the 'secret sauce' in the 10 000 words a day recipe. Rachel Aaron did some deep analysis of her productive writing days and compared these to the occasional not-so-productive days. She was able to write even more than 10 000 words when she was writing scenes she had been 'dying to write' – she called these 'the candy bar scenes'. On days where she found it hard to muster 5000 words she was bored with what she was writing.

In the fiction world the answer to Rachel's dilemma was simple – make the boring scenes more interesting!

Unfortunately in Thesis World this is not always possible. There will always be parts that are functional and unexciting. I call these the 'dry toast' sections – you need to do a lot of unproductive chewing before you can swallow what has been written.

There's a term that describes this process in gamer culture: 'grinding'. Grinding is being forced to perform the same action over and over again before you can 'level up' in the game and get more powers/weapons/armour or whatever. The level up is the pay-off.

One of the most genius ideas Liam and Peta incorporated into the Thesis Boot Camp was the squeezy Lego-style blocks. We give these out for each 5000 words written in a particular colour order: green, blue, red and gold. The blocks clip together to make a little Lego 'wall' that the students can display at their writing station. When first presented with the idea of the blocks the students laugh, but all too soon they are typing furiously with single-minded purpose – to get the next block. We have a little ceremony every time someone gets a block, clapping them as they walk up to write their name on the board. It's cheesy, but it works to turn writing from a source of pain to a celebration. So think about how to reward yourself for every 5000 words written.

WHY YOU MIGHT BE 'STUCK'

In high school I had a German history teacher who would talk about the Second World War like he was a proud German soldier. At first his performance was funny. In his hands every Allied victory became a loss; every weakness of the Allies was celebrated and German losses lamented. But as the year went on, and we learned about the extermination of the Jewish people and others, I became increasingly outraged and confused. My teacher seemed to regard these atrocities lightly. Was it just perverse admiration for the German war machine? Or was he some kind of escaped Nazi war criminal?!

I began to dread history classes. For a long time I didn't say anything because I was a Good Girl. It was not my place to question the teacher, who was clearly an expert on the subject. But one day I just couldn't take it any more. I finally put my hand up and inquired, in a trembling voice, why he thought the Germans were so great. He just looked at me silently, which goaded me into anger. I started yelling at him. 'The Allies weren't hopeless! They won the war, after all! Are you some kind of nut job?!'

I'd never, never yelled at a teacher before. I couldn't

quite believe what I was doing, but the rage felt good. He stayed silent until I finished ranting. I was worried about being in trouble then, but he looked amused – and maybe a little bit relieved. By way of an answer, he started telling us his story of fleeing from Europe with his parents at the start of the war.

Then he told us he was a Jew. He told us he was lying about everything. He hated the German war machine because most of his family had been killed.

I was shocked and deeply confused. It must have shown on my face, because he paused and looked at me expectantly. Under the pressure of his stare I blurted out: 'Now I know you have lied … how do I know anything you say is true?' He smiled and answered with a question that has haunted me ever since.

'How do you know anything said to you by a teacher is true?'

This question hit me right in the stomach. I was 16 years old, but (sadly) this is the first time I realised a teacher could consciously choose – or even be forced – to lie. Simultaneously, I realised how conditioned I was to swallowing what my teachers told me, unquestioningly. I can honestly say this moment changed my life. I felt liberated. I didn't have to believe my teachers anymore!

But for the rest of high school and for a long time afterwards, I found learning exhausting and sometimes deeply unsettling. Reluctantly (I was 16, after all, and wanted to be thinking about boys at that point) I started to question everything anyone told me – including my parents. Did they *know* what they were saying was true, or were they simply taking it on faith? Were they trying to trick me? This led to a lot of tension at home, believe me.

Professor Jan Meyer, professor of education, would say that when I realised that teachers could lie, I encountered, and crossed over, a 'threshold concept'. The complex insight about teaching and power, once grasped, was unforgettable. It made me see the world in a new and transformed way. As is common with this kind of learning threshold, before I crossed over I had been 'stuck', unable even to give voice to my questions. After I crossed the threshold, the insight I gained was integrative. It caused other knowledge I had been exposed to to fall into place: knowledge about history, the school system, my place in it and even the nature of truth and belief, good and evil. But this changed knowledge led to a changed sense of self. I was no longer a compliant teenager. I had started on the journey to being a questioning, independent adult. Learning was no longer routine, but question-filled, troublesome and uncertain.

Being 'stuck' is a common experience for PhD students and researchers alike. It often manifests as difficulty in writing. When you can't work out why you are stuck, or how to get over it, you could be facing a threshold concept without realising it. Researchers Margaret Kiley and Gina Wisker have studied threshold learning in a PhD study and came to the remarkable conclusion that certain PhD threshold concepts are consistent across all disciplines. These manifest as a common set of struggles:

- the struggle to understand that a thesis is a claim or defence of a position, not just a collection of work you have done or a way of proving existing beliefs
- the struggle to be able to articulate a position on 'the literature' or locate the work you are doing within it
- the struggle to develop a theory or a model which allows the findings to be used, or applied to other cases.

I think threshold concepts can manifest as modest, mundane affairs. You may become stuck because you need to unlearn certain ways of doing things. For instance, most of us have learned to write in linear ways. Trying to plan out your whole thesis can make you feel disheartened at the size and difficulty of the task. But you don't have to start at the beginning – you can write the conclusion first if you want to. Writing a thesis is more like developing a picture in a darkroom than it is like putting sheets of paper through a typewriter.

A lot of the advice on doing a PhD, and doing research generally, does not recognise these conceptual blocks. Many treat doing a thesis like a project which has to be 'managed', not a difficult and troublesome learning process. Research degree learning involves encountering and changing some deeply habitual ways of operating and thinking. The project management approach doesn't always work. Unfortunately, when it doesn't, it's all too easy to blame yourself for not working efficiently rather than recognising that 'efficient' doesn't look the same for everyone.

I think the idea of 'threshold concepts' helps us think more positively about 'being stuck'. Being stuck can be a sign you are learning something important – or maybe not. One good way to move forward is to ask yourself: 'Is there anything I need to unlearn?' Now there's a concept to sit with.

● ● ● EMAIL, SHE WROTE

Email ... blessing or curse of contemporary academic
life? Recently I received a letter that touched on a sore
topic for many PhD students and academics: the unanswered email.

> Hi Inger
>
> I have a question for you about email contact with
> supervisors.
>   ... I rely on email and phone for a lot of my
> discussion with my supervisor. I find it difficult
> when I don't get a reply to an email, and I'm
> not always sure what the correct response is. For
> example, I emailed 3 days ago asking to set up a
> phone call. I haven't heard back, and past experience
> suggests I may not.
>   So do I email again? How long do I wait before
> emailing? ... Sometimes when I do re-email, it
> turns out he's been doing Very Important Things
> and I feel like I've been hassling him by contacting
> too much! Any advice please?
>
> Anonymous Emailer

We've all had the experience of urgent emails going unanswered. Many people in academia, myself included, are drowning in email. The problem with email is that it becomes a 'to-do' list made for you by other people – a to-do list that never ends. In this case, Anonymous Emailer's research supervisor had probably opened and closed her email without answering it, thinking, 'I'll deal with this one later, when I have time'.

We all imagine we will have spare time in our future to attend to deferred tasks, but if you're a busy person spare time will always be in desperately short supply. Emails like this tend to get ignored because they are a call to action that is too complex to carry out straight away. All emails are a call to action of some sort. Sometimes the required action is a simple answer to the sender's question: 'yes', 'no', 'good', 'bad', 'maybe'. Other times the sender urgently wants an explanation of what has happened, or should happen.

If the call to action is clear and easy to do, the email usually gets answered, probably reasonably promptly. Other emails ask the receiver to take an action, or a sequence of actions, before answering. These are more likely to get deferred. For example, an email might ask me what I think about something, or to provide information that is not ready to hand. This email asking a supervisor for a phone call is a good example. You think all that's required is a simple response – 'yes' or 'no' – but it's not that simple because the action involves calendar management.

Like this supervisor, my calendar is always very full. If someone wants to see me I must pull my calendar up and scan for gaps. Meetings disrupt focus, so I like to gang them together. I'll need to find a day that has some meetings in it already, then I have to calculate the full effect of the proposed meeting on the rest of my schedule, balancing each request with preparation time, travel time and the likelihood that other meetings will run over time. Calendar requests are especially problematic if the meeting is with more than one person. First I must find a couple of potential times and put placeholders in. Then I must wait for a response from two or more people. If none of the times I've suggested work, I must delete the placeholders, find new ones … you see the problem. One email can quickly become 20 as people try to move their schedules around. It's not unusual for an hour of work time to be eaten in tiny chunks before a group meeting can be scheduled.

The problem is, every time we defer responding to an email we start accumulating a time debt. Deferred emails pile up like autumn leaves. This student's email about a phone call might have moved to page 2 and have a mountain of other, seemingly more pressing, tiny tasks ahead of it. Unbeknownst to the poor student, their email has become digital fertiliser. Sooner or later you will have to take what blogger Katherine Firth calls 'the electronic walk of shame' to the bottom of your inbox. All the time you 'saved' by ignoring the problem must now be spent.

Email is truly one of contemporary life's contradictions: at the same time a wonderful invention and a sure and steady productivity killer. I have exactly the opposite problem with email than the one the student is experiencing above. I always answer emails, mostly promptly. Unlike much of my other work, email is a clear-cut, process-driven and achievable part of my job. I will privilege email over more important tasks, like writing and reading books. A lot of people say the trick to managing an email addiction like mine is to only do it at specific times, but I've tried that and it doesn't work for me. I suspect the full-blown email addict needs a regular hit and standard time-management strategies simply aren't going to cut it. What you need is a system. Here's mine.

Treat email like doing the dishes

Keeping on top of your email is a task more like housework than letter writing. The bulging inbox is like a dirty kitchen full of guilt and missed opportunities – it's hard to cook when there's a mess. I have cultivated two modes of email attention to deal with the mess, which (following the Lifehack blog, <www.lifehack.org>) I call 'passing through' and 'eating the frogs'.

The aim of passing through is to handle each new email as lightly as possible and move on. If an email needs more than two minutes to read and respond to, it gets moved to the program OmniFocus2 for later attention. Each of these emails is a 'frog', which has to be eaten at some point (I'll get to that in a moment). The passing through mode is like giving the kitchen what my mother called 'a surface clean'. Email is dealt with continuously, with minimal effort and your addiction can become a strength; your inbox will never have more than three or four things in it. What used to be a laborious chore becomes a soothing break from thinking, rather than an interruption to your focus.

Stop filing emails – process them instead

I used to have an email filing system related to projects and to people. It took so long to file anything I wouldn't bother half the time, so my inbox was so crowded I had to use the search function to find things. Slowly I realised all I needed was the search function. An email has two states – active, or dealt with. I put all the ones I have dealt with in a box called 'archive'. I've added two subfolders to this over time: one for tax receipts and the other for nice feedback. I can't tell you how much time

I saved by giving up filing. More importantly, I've saved cognitive effort I can now devote to other things. I know it makes many people anxious to think that their email is not 'tidy', but 'tidy' does not mean 'filed', it means 'processed'. Trust me and try it for a while. You'll find it's better to let the computer find the email than look for it yourself.

Develop a terse yet friendly email style

Many people don't know how to write effective emails. This is probably a topic for another time, but I think it's worth mentioning here that emails should be as brief as possible. Try to say what you want from the person, or would like them to do, within the first line or two. I usually write quite abrupt emails. This is contrary to my urge to be polite, but I write for a living and only have so many words per day to spend on emails.

Eat the frogs

To make this simple system work you need a program to hold all those deferred emails – the frogs. I use Omni-Focus2, which is connected to my mailbox and calendar. It's a Mac-only program, but Asana, which is a cloud-based product, is similar and works on the PC or the Mac. These programs work like a ticket system on a computer helpdesk, allowing you to store, keep track of and schedule all of the tasks that emails present to you. Email changes from a to-do list made by other people to a to-do list you make yourself.

Once transferred to OmniFocus2, each email becomes an action that is filed under a project and a context. A project or a context can be anything you like – they are just two ways of looking at the same information. I take 'projects' to mean areas of my activities like writing, teaching and events management; 'contexts' tend to be actions or people.

Take the example from above – an email from a student asking for a panel meeting and suggesting a couple of convenient times. I put the times the student has suggested aside in my diary and immediately respond to the student saying I am on it, so they don't have to chase me. I then assign a project (research supervision) and context (the student's name) and set a date and time that I will come back to it. Then I promptly forget about it until the program reminds me. I then reach out on email to the other research supervisors, making a note on the original email so I remember where I was up to. I then move the email to a different context (waiting). I set a time on how long I will wait for a response from my colleagues and forget about it again. One of two things happens at this point: I hear back, or the program reminds me I have waited long enough for an answer.

Only then will I pick up the phone. Once I know what time will suit everyone, I send an email to the student to confirm our agreement then tick the task off.

It sounds like a lot of work when I explain it like this, but trust me that it's not because the machine is doing all the remembering for me. I just have to respond at the appropriate moments. Being able to annotate each email with notes about the actions you have taken means you don't repeat steps, or look disorganised by asking people twice for the same thing. It also helps when people in administration roles in your university aren't responsive to requests for information or services – a constant problem for me, no matter where I have worked. A terse 'I emailed you about this matter on the 13th of April and again two weeks later' is usually enough of a signal that you are that rarest of creatures: an academic who is frighteningly organised and there-fore not to be messed with.

So that's all there is to it, Grasshoppers. Of course, there are some days I have to spend more time on email than I would like, but at least the task is simplified. No system is perfect, but I have been working diligently on this problem for ten years and now feel I have the prob-lem solved – at least, as much as it ever will be.

5

BEING EMPLOYED
(OR NOT ...)

I graduated from architecture school in 1996, 25 years old and poor.

I had no trouble finding work at the tail end of a recession because I was really good at something that many other people at the time were not: computer-aided design (CAD). As some of you may remember, computers back then were a lot less friendly than they are now. Many people in the architecture offices I worked in found it difficult to get acquainted. The slow invasion of silicon resulted in the loss of many people from the profession. Architectural practice did not help fill my coffers and it was not as fun as I had imagined. I spent a lot of time reminding myself that I was investing in my future. My employer told me my computer skills were non-essential 'icing on the cake' for their clients. I accepted this until one day when I happened upon an invoice on the printer. Clients were being charged

$250 an hour for my 'icing' when I was being paid about $10. I quit and decided to turn my mad computing skills into cold hard cash by working with a big developer. Colour me surprised when I literally doubled my income overnight. My peers, thoroughly socialised by the architectural profession, told me I was a sell-out, but I didn't care.

I am struck by the similarity of this experience with the trajectory of my academic career, which started around 15 years ago. I spent the first part of my academic career scraping around on the margins. I spent a lot of time, as I worked and studied for my PhD, reminding myself I was investing in the future. Again, my only 'edge' in this competitive environment was my computing skills.

For a long time, academia has been slowly invaded by technology. Like those architects in offices in the 1990s, most academics have acquired familiarity with technology but relatively few of us really love it. Only some of my colleagues operate blogs or engage with people on Twitter. Until recently, people were slow to adopt the free, cloud-based tools and technologies that make academic work so much faster. I still think these tools are underutilised. There is another kind of 'digital divide', one which threatens to leave some people behind. I'll take myself as an example.

The Thesis Whisperer has been running for some

seven years. It's got solid niche appeal as a survival blog aimed at research students and has been much more successful than I expected. Thanks to easy access via social media, my work has been featured in the mainstream media, in newspapers, magazines and on the radio. As a result I have been invited to give keynote talks, flown around the country and internationally to talk about my work and approached to write books like this one. In short, I have had access to opportunities usually reserved for more experienced players. It would take me at least 20 years, maybe more, to achieve this kind of status and recognition through the normal academic fame channels of citations and conference attendances.

I still write academic works for journals, of course – I realise that my institution and the majority of people in my research field won't take me seriously if I don't. There's some pleasure in the difficulty of scholarly work but I prefer writing blog posts, and not just because they are easier. In my work with PhD students, blog posts do more than journal papers. Most PhD students will never bother to read Alison Lee's most excellent work on research student identities, but I can translate these ideas into easily digestible chunks and link through to the original texts for those who want more. I can boost the worthy work of others and introduce new ideas.

My ability to do research has been turbo-charged by contact with others through social media. In fact, I get very frustrated when people tell me I waste my time on Twitter. By being connected I gain as well as give. As a result of hanging out online, chatting and sharing for the last seven years or so, I can tap an international, professional network which might rival those of some senior professors I know. Those professors have spent 20 years writing, working and flying around to conferences to develop their network; I have sat on my behind and talked to people online. I wonder if some of my fellow early career researchers dislike me and my growing profile. Are they, like my architecture peers so long ago, sneering at my 'non-scholarly' work? They rarely say anything, but some friendly senior colleagues have expressed concern at the time I take out from publishing in conventional forums to blog, tweet and otherwise hang out on social media. I take their point, but stopping now seems like the riskier strategy.

A lot of academics and research students I talk to seem to be very hesitant to jump in and give this whole 'web thing' a try. Again, I think age is a factor, but it's not the whole story. Some of the most connected academics I know are in their fifties and sixties and there are a significant number of us rocking it out in our forties. Perhaps the collective nature of some academic cultures, like science, work against those seeking to have an individual voice and profile before they have 'done their time' at the bottom of the pile. However, I fret about the vast majority of early career academics who remain but ghostly presences online and don't take advantage of what is on offer, if only for boosting their research productivity.

The posts featured in this chapter speak to my ongoing interest in the connections between networking, employability and all things money related. My own experience with long periods of underemployment in academia motivates my current research, which I regularly publish on the blog. My work in this space often unsettles people, perhaps because there is an unspoken, middle-class rule in academia forbidding the discussion of money. I start the chapter with two posts about academic job hunting which are based on my own experience and backed up by ongoing research into the nature of the academic job market. In What's Your Edge? I discuss the importance of distinguishing yourself in a competitive job market. The Existential PhD Crisis addresses the mismatch between the PhD and the nature of academic work. The PhD experience can be relatively solitary compared to the constant 'hustle' of being a full-time academic. I follow this up with Academic on the Inside?, which starts to address the cultural issues that PhD graduates must face if they want to get into a non-academic career – are we bred to be too aggressive for many corporate cultures? The next three posts deal with networking – a concept that is often presented quite instrumentally. I look for cultural angles and give out some actionable advice on how to deal with the mundane problems of the conference dinner table. If You Blog, Will You Lose Your Job? was written in a froth of rage about Latrobe University's ill-treatment of an academic who dared to speak up on important subjects. There is still much work to be done to protect academic freedom to blog. In Niche Marketing for Academics I lay out a strategy to help you boost your published papers online. Finally, in #fifoacademic I meditate on some of the gender issues that often mean women face a more difficult task in establishing an academic career than men.

I hope these posts provide some strategies and tactics for all the different stages of your academic career – and beyond.

HOW TO GET A JOB IN ACADEMIA

The usual advice for PhD students wanting a career in academia when they finish boils down to 'Publish early, publish often'. However, after reading some research from the National Tertiary Education Union (NTEU), I think we should approach this advice with caution. It seems that most academics who get permanent positions do teaching and research. Being 'one-dimensional' – that is, just a researcher or just a teacher – is the surest road to marginal employment. Academia is not a meritocracy. It is a workplace like any other, but perhaps with more than your average number of delicate egos and competing interests. Some people will tell you there is an element of luck involved and that you don't have much control. But do you want to know what I think?

Screw luck.

I'm a firm believer in making your own luck. After years in the trenches as a casual lecturer and numerous unsuccessful job interviews I finally achieved my ambition of being a full-time academic. Here are the five most important things I learned along the way.

Get the right kind of teaching experience

Research by the NTEU showed that 80 per cent of undergraduate teaching is done by casuals, so there's plenty of work around. This should allow you to have choice in the classes you teach, so be strategic: diversify. This will enable you to show future employers you can teach across a range of subjects and year levels. Try not to get stuck in a specialist role, but, if you do, make sure it's a technical side of the discipline as these are usually the hardest roles to fill.

Be generous to other casual lecturers. Have a list of names to recommend to your school contact if you can't fill a role. You will find other casuals generally return the favour, either next semester or even later in your career. Having people feel well disposed to you is a good way to grow your professional network. Your role as 'finder' is valuable to permanent staff members too, who may pass on your details to other staff members who are looking for warm bodies. I felt like a bit of a pimp sometimes, but I did get to know many people within my institution this way. And I found out it's true what they say: who you know really is more important than what you know.

Get 'backstage' whenever possible

Try to gain some administrative experience. Volunteer to take a leading role, like that of head tutor, and attend all the staff meetings you can. Offer to join the ethics committee, or, even better, the research committee. Watching academics in these 'backstage' activities is very instructive – but keep your mouth shut until you get a sense of how it all works. When you are visible 'backstage', it helps the academics in the school to view you as a colleague, not a student. It puts you in a position to ask for job references or career advice. If you are lucky, you may get advance notice of upcoming positions, either at your institution or at others.

If you can, work the 'coat-tails' method

A couple of times I was shortlisted for a position but beaten by people – ok, men – who were less qualified than me, but had been research assistants at one time for powerful professors in the department. I'm not too clear on how the research assistant to full-time staff member transition works, probably because I am not a man, but clearly it does.

Is there a magical formula to cultivating the favour of powerful professors? I think there must be. The relationships I've seen are deep and often they go back to undergraduate years. Perhaps the powerful professor sees in the protege a version of their younger self? Since most of the powerful are still 'pale and male', it's going to be harder for those of us who aren't ... or maybe I am just being cynical? I have met plenty of people who are 'stuck' in the role of protege and unable to escape, so perhaps it's a risky strategy too.

Look for 'the adjacent possible'

I taught casually while I worked as an architect, so I had a lot of teaching experience before I developed a serious ambition to be an academic. Although I was very successful at getting jobs when I was an architect, clearly the criteria for becoming an architecture academic were different. After a series of unsuccessful and demoralising job interviews, I had to face facts: architecture departments were just not that into me.

I liked the university lifestyle too much to leave, so I started to look for what Steven Johnson calls 'the adjacent possible'. In my case, this meant the so-called 'professional roles' which were available in the central administrative units. To my surprise, I had the skill set and background to be a contender, so when a job came up I had a go, not really caring if I got it or not. I didn't get it, but I came very close, which inspired me to continue looking for non-architecture opportunities.

My first job as a research educator was offered to me as a six-week casual contract for two days a week. I figured: what have I got to lose? It was academic, but it wasn't architecture, therefore I might learn something different. I reasoned that this might tip me over the line next time a professional role came up. Twelve years later here I am, an associate professor in research education and as happy as a clam. To paraphrase the Rolling Stones, you can't always get what you want, but if you are open to other possibilities, you just might get what you need. Broaden your horizons about what 'being an academic' might mean. Look for an adjacent discipline, or even country, if you don't mind moving. Have a look at some of those 'quasi-academic' roles: many are well paid and allow you to use your research skills without the pressure to publish.

Remember – it's 'co-operition', not co-operation ...

Great – you've finally been shortlisted for an interview! Half the battle is won, but remember what I said about fragile egos? Your researcher talents can be an asset, but they are also a potential threat to your future colleagues. Read the CVs of all the permanent staff members carefully and download a selection of their papers. Ask yourself: where do I fit in? Who can I work with? What can I offer that's slightly different to what is already here, but clearly useful? Find ways to present yourself as filling a gap in the current staff profile, not overlapping.

I wish you all the best with your academic dreams.

 ## WHAT DO ACADEMIC EMPLOYERS WANT?

My friend and colleague Rachael Pitt, known on Twitter as @thefellowette, has followed a conventional academic career path. By 'conventional' I don't mean that she finished her PhD, accepted a permanent position as a lecturer and has worked at the same university ever since. Oh no, no, no – that was a conventional academic career back in 1980. Now we have the Academic Hunger Games and the 'new normal' academic has done a decade or so of adjunct teaching work, and/or a ragtag bunch of jobs that lasted anywhere from a week to three years. I did the former; Rachael did the latter.

For the last ten years Rachael has had what some call 'a portfolio career', but what is more accurately called a 'post-post-postdoc'. There are some unexpected upsides to being the new normal academic, at least for the people who survive. All of Rachael's jobs have been loosely in our mutual field of expertise (research education), but all of them have required her to learn new things fast and work out how to function in different university settings. As a consequence, she's a highly skilled and adaptable researcher and a great collaborator who never has trouble finding work. I think of Rachael as a one-woman academic SWAT team, able to work both the academic and professional side of the university fence. Starting a new undergraduate research program with only a vague idea of where it's all headed? Rachael's your woman. Your reliable postgrad admin officer had to leave to have a baby early and there are no handover notes? Call Rachael – she'll keep the show on the road. You want her to move cities to join your research project? Make her an offer she can't refuse!

Mobility is the glue that holds a portfolio career together. After her PhD Rachael moved to a different city every couple of years, finding new places to live and learning new public transport systems while wrangling a growing pile of stuff. In every new city she had to make new friends. Like many academics, Rachael identifies as an introvert, but I would argue her mobility experience turned her into one of the best academic networkers I know. Most of my networking consists of hanging around on Twitter, but Rachael is far more hard core. We know each other because she cold called a colleague of mine, explained that she had just moved to Melbourne and suggested we all have lunch.

From this humble beginning a beautiful academic friendship unfolded.

Until recently, Rachael was the perfect worker for the bad boyfriend university, always ready and able to find the next gig. But the hyper-mobile academic life is physically and emotionally taxing. Rachael is a generous friend, a fun aunt and a loving daughter in addition to being an academic. All this moving around for an academic career was very isolating. Building a new relationship with a life partner, or even a pet, was difficult. I'm very happy to report that in 2015 Rachael got married to a lovely man and moved back to her home state of Queensland, where she can play with her nieces and nephews whenever she wants.

Of course, she found a job in three seconds flat too.

I wanted to tell you Rachael's academic story because we recently wrote an academic paper together which was deeply informed by her hyper-mobile portfolio career. We called it 'Academic superheroes: a critical analysis of academic job descriptions'. In it we analysed the text of job ads to see if there was evidence of this 'new normal' academic life.

Rachael came up with the idea for this research in 2013, when we were sitting on the couch drinking tea and eating chips. At the time, Rachael was nearing the end of yet another contract. Funding was running out and she was about to be in the wind yet again.

She started telling me about the difficulties and general tediousness of the academic job application process.

In Australia, academic employers list jobs with a short piece of text and a list of 'key selection criteria'. The applicant is meant to respond to each of these key selection criteria in a lengthy cover letter, in addition to submitting their CV (an epic task in its own right). Each application is bespoke, so every rejection letter represents hours, sometimes weeks, of work. Rachael told me that some of her written responses to ads were more than 15 pages long. During this tedious process, Rachael noticed that many academic job ads seemed downright impossible to live up to. Many listed conflicting, ambiguous criteria that were impossible to evidence. For instance, one ad asked for 'a PhD and evidence towards submitting for your PhD in psychology [sic]' as the first key selection criterion, immediately followed by 'evidence of expertise in psychology?' Doesn't one imply the other? And how do you evidence a statement like: 'Effective organisational skills to plan and organise work to meet competing deadlines and ability to work independently with minimal supervision, showing initiative and flexibility'? I guess you could write something about how awesome you are, but why should someone believe you? Wouldn't it be better just to ask your referees?

No wonder many PhD students who are exploring the academic job market are confused and demoralised.

In her last research gun-for-hire job, Rachael had uncovered evidence that academic employers were unhappy with PhD graduates after they hired them. This finding is both odd and ironic: academics design the PhD experience, put students through it, evaluate the outcomes and then employ around 40 per cent of the graduates. How is it possible they are unhappy?! But the finding makes a bit more sense when you think about what you do to get a PhD. While there is some innovation around the edges, most PhD programs still ask the student to produce a long thesis dissertation. This document is evidence you can think, be creative and write academically. It is decidedly *not* evidence that you can teach, sit on committees, write peer reviews, design curriculum or any of the other myriad tasks that are part of a large and complicated university bureau-cracy. In her PhD thesis, my friend Mary-Helen Ward accused the PhD of having an 'accidental pedagogy' and I think she's right.

Rachael and I started connecting these impossible job ad texts with what is being taught in the PhD – or, more precisely, what is *not* explicitly taught in the PhD. Here are just two of the things that we discuss in the paper.

Academic employers want people who play well with others

It is possible to be a clever, productive academic and be an asshole at the same time. If you are well entrenched somewhere, management might be too scared to get rid of you, but watch out if you have a reputation for being an asshole before you step through the door. In fact, many of the ads we looked at showed academic employers want team players. They called for people who would adjust to the flow of work and help others, especially with respect (surprisingly) to the emotional life of the department. Job ads mentioned things like counselling students and even other staff members in times of crisis. Other ads signalled that they want academics who treat their non-academic colleagues with respect and courtesy. It's been my experience that once a shortlist is created it is discussed informally. Actually, let's not sugar-coat it: people will try to find out the gossip about everyone on that list. Your reputation is always in the process of being made in every interaction you have. Don't ignore the administrators! Good admin people know everybody, are highly trusted and excellent sources of gossip. If you are the type of person who is 'too busy' to treat everyone with respect, regardless of status, you might be kicked off the shortlist before you even knew you were on it.

Academic employers want your network – but probably not for the reasons you think

A solidly built peer-to-peer academic network is like gold. Hopefully you start building this network as a student and keep adding to it through your whole career. Through your peer network you will hear about upcoming job opportunities, will receive warnings about funding cuts and gather other valuable intel. But your future academic employer wants your professional connections outside of the academy too. This is especially true in practice-based disciplines such as architecture, nursing, education and the like. Your employer will want you to use the people you know in all kinds of ways. For instance, connections to the outside will help you place undergraduates in intern programs and raise money, either through consulting or philanthropy. Pursuing a non-academic career path after a PhD is often seen as a road that leads away from academia permanently, but after looking at all these job ads I'm not so sure this is true. I suspect that if you go 'outside' and actively maintain your ties, by collaborating with academics, supervising students or writing papers, you might find yourself in an excellent competitive position should you decide to come back in a few years. The pay tends to be better outside, though, so you might decide you never want to come back!

The skills academic employers are looking for are not necessarily part of the PhD experience by default. You will learn more about doing academic work by taking an active part in the life of the department than by writing your dissertation – for example, acting as the student representative on a committee and watching how people behave when the students aren't around is certainly an education in academic politics! Don't deny yourself this learning by focussing on the research alone – there's so much more to learn about this academic life.

WHAT'S YOUR EDGE?: THE ADVANTAGE OF AN ACADEMIC USP

When the mainstream press bothers to talk about academia, they always paint us as being in some kind of crisis. Either it's about the parlous state of the academic job market or the pointlessness of doing a PhD. These articles are naturally depressing for anyone currently enrolled in a PhD, but are things really as bad as they seem?

There is very little data on what happens to PhD graduates in the workforce. Currently the best data we have in Australia is from Graduate Careers Australia, which shows that 60 per cent of graduates now work outside of academia. The median wage three years after graduation is $91 600, the full-time employment rate is just on 90 per cent and the unemployment rate is around 2 per cent. If the aim of the doctorate is to produce gainfully employed graduates (you could debate this point, but I won't just for the moment), the PhD is doing its job.

What doesn't show up in this data is whether people are doing work they want to do, or if they have as much work as they would like. I suspect many PhD graduates are working in other fields or working many casual jobs at once. It's a sad fact of life that we can't all get what we want. If your aim is to be a scholar of medieval history, for example, there is a vanishingly small chance you will actually achieve this aim. Most of us will have to do work that is only indirectly related (if at all) to our PhD topic – but is that such a bad thing?

Very few of my friends and family are doing what they originally trained to do. Take as just one example my sister, who studied to be a graphic designer. She worked in beauty products and publishing before she became a manager of an art department in a large software development company. She then started running a graphic design school with around 40 teaching staff and thousands of students. This all sounds ordinary, until

I tell you that the academic program Anitra manages has no classrooms, corridors, bathrooms or any of the other paraphernalia we associate with academia. Anitra works for the Academy of Art, which will be familiar to anyone who lives in San Francisco as they seem to own much of the downtown area. While there is a face-to-face graphic design program located on the SF campus, Anitra runs the cyber campus, which has thousands of paying students located all around the world, from Brazil to outer Mongolia. This totally online graphic design program turns over millions of dollars a year – but you probably have never heard of it. Anitra works from a study in her house in Melbourne, Australia. Thanks to the internet, location just isn't what it used to be.

As academic and productivity expert Cal Newport says in his fantastic book *So Good They Can't Ignore You*, passion can follow skill. When we are young, we are encouraged to 'live the dream that is you' and follow our passions towards a dream job. Newport argues we should do precisely the opposite. The more skilled you get at something, he contends, the more you will come to enjoy your work. I would encourage down-hearted doctoral students to give this idea some serious consideration.

I am fond of saying to anyone who will listen: 'No one wakes up one day and says "I want to be a research educator".' I certainly didn't plan to be a Thesis

Whisperer – I wanted to be an architect. I trained in architecture for 12 years, but when I couldn't get a job in my field I had to open my mind and see what else was available. Like many of my other colleagues, I ended up in research education by accident. I say 'accident' because I think the only reason I got my first job in research education was that I could use Blackboard, RMIT University's learning management system. I didn't love Blackboard, but I liked the conversations with students I had there. I became interested in online education and technology, which eventually led me to blogging and, well ... here I am. Passion follows skill. I love my career and can't imagine doing anything else, but I can imagine doing it in other places. I try to remember that my career is what I do; my job is what I'm paid to do.

You're probably wondering exactly what my point is here. Well, in order for passion to follow skill you need to create the opportunity and space for it to happen. One way you can do this is to concentrate on your 'unique selling proposition' (USP). According to Wikipedia, in marketing parlance a USP is a 'unique benefit exhibited by a company, service, product or brand that enables it to stand out from competitors' – that is, the product has a benefit for consumers that the competition doesn't.

In the competitive academic job market, it sometimes helps to run in the opposite direction to the crowd. If everyone else is concentrating on understanding and articulating the finer points of Derrida and making heady theoretical arguments, go and get some statistical training. Work out how to use a pivot table (they are amazing), then come back and see if you can apply the pivot table skills to a problem in your field. Likewise, it is well known that many people are attracted to science because they don't like writing. So why not concentrate during your PhD on developing your writing skills? Get really good at it – specifically, get fast at it (this is just a matter of the right kind of practice). Get so good and so fast at writing that people want you on their team because your writing is your USP.

In short: become known for doing something that not too many other people in your field can do. This is your edge. Use it and be open to where these skills might take you. (You might not have any idea where that is yet, but have faith.) To make the best use of your USP you have to find ways to tell the right people exactly how good you are ... but that's a post for another time.

So I will leave you with these questions: what is your edge? Can you talk about your USP confidently? If you don't have a USP, what is everyone else doing and how can you be different?

THE EXISTENTIAL PHD CRISIS

I'm constantly surprised at how doing a PhD can trigger a full-blown existential crisis in otherwise quite rational and well-balanced people. Most of the time my job involves helping people through such crises, but sometimes the crisis is a good thing. Sometimes a crisis is your subconscious speaking and you should listen.

Recently a student, let's call her Lisa, came to see me because she was wondering whether she should quit her PhD. In an effort to understand what was happening, I asked her to tell me why she had started the degree in the first place. Lisa explained her situation as one of inertia. After finishing undergraduate studies in the humanities, she'd only been able to find clerical work. After a year or two of being bored out of her mind, she went back to the place where she had always been intellectually happy – the university. Lisa was attracted to the research work of the PhD, but only had vague thoughts about what she would do after it.

As Music for Deckchairs blogger Kate Bowles once remarked: a PhD is the worst back-up plan ever. Joining the department enabled Lisa to come face-to-face with the reality of academic work, specifically how little of it resembles the life of the mind she'd imagined.

Academic life is no longer one of leisured reflection (if indeed it ever was). Teaching, committee meetings and marking take up most of our time. Research happens in snatched moments, or on the weekend. Lots of that research time is spent writing the next grant application. The employment is not secure, either. You are likely to be on short-term contacts and maintaining your professional network is crucial to getting that next job.

Building networks involves interacting with a large variety of people through collaboration, conference travel and even (my favourite) social media. This was Lisa's issue: she identified as an introvert and the people work of academia just didn't appeal. I don't really believe in the introvert/extrovert thing, but if I have to commit to one or the other then I'm definitely an extrovert. While I see social media as fun, Lisa sees it as a boring waste of time. I love teaching; Lisa likes nothing better than being alone with her books. In fact, Lisa admitted that public speaking makes her anxious. She has some close friends in academia, but collaborating or co-writing is just not her thing. I suspect Lisa's worst nightmare is to be trapped in a three-hour committee meeting.

Academia might not be a good career choice for Lisa, but that's not a deal-breaker for the PhD itself. Sixty per cent of graduates leave academia at the end of the PhD and they do all sorts of things. I talked enthusiastically about how much more money non-academic doctors earn and rattled off a list of other jobs Lisa could do, but she looked unimpressed. All of those jobs I mentioned involved dealing with lots of people and she wasn't into it.

We sat in silence for a while, then Lisa made a statement which made everything clear: 'I really want to work with plants, not people'. I was a little taken aback, but when Lisa started talking about her secret ambition to open a nursery she became truly animated. I suggested that it was perfectly ok to quit and do that instead – you don't need to have a PhD to run a nursery. Sure, she'd wasted a year or two, but as that old proverb goes 'The best time to plant a tree is 20 years ago. The second-best time is now'.

Whenever I validate a student's desire to quit, they will immediately start to back-pedal, and Lisa was no exception. She immediately listed a bunch of reasons to keep going, all of which were about what other people would think of her if she gave up. I'm not trained to unpick the workings of the mind and motivation, so I sent her straight back to counselling. I hope she works it out.

A PhD-induced existential crisis doesn't have to come from within – it can be provoked by people around you. This kind of crisis is more like emotional contagion than a message from your subconscious. For example, the other week I got an email from a student, let's call him Ching. Ching was rattled because of a conversation he'd had with a group of academics from his department at lunch. 'We were talking about my project', he said, 'and one of them, who is normally super positive and super supportive, started asking me questions about what I was trying to achieve with my project, which I thought I was answering OK, but it quickly became quite aggressive and confrontational – she was asking me why I was doing something that wasn't going to help anyone, or make any difference.'

Oh boy.

The last thing you need while you are up to your elbows in a PhD is for someone to say something like that. In this case, it probably says more about that academic's state of mind than Ching's work, but it still stings. Look – it's unlikely that your PhD will change anything about the world. Mine didn't make much of a ripple, but that doesn't mean it was a waste of time. It depends on what you think is the most important product of a PhD: the dissertation document or the person.

Most of the time I prefer to keep my focus on the person. What did they learn about the topic? Are they now more empowered in work? In life? How can the knowledge and skills they have developed be transferred to another setting or problem?

Personally, my readings in material semiotics and assemblage thinking help me cope with committees and paperwork. I'm more patient with processes because I understand exactly why we find change hard inside a bureaucracy. My reading on habitus and cultural capital helps me understand how PhD students adapt (or don't) to life inside the academy. With that knowledge I can create novel ways to assist them, through programs and interventions.

My knowledge of research methods in gesture research is not much good to my present work in PhD employability, but I understand the principles of how methods produce knowledge and I can read really fast. But if I had to name the very best outcome of the PhD (besides being greeted with 'Welcome back, Dr Mewburn' while boarding aeroplanes) is that I am not afraid to appear stupid.

When I discover my ignorance, I know how to fix it. I'll just research the shit out of it. People should fear my mad skills of research. When my last landlord tried to deduct money from our bond for the state of the garden at the end of the lease, I researched the law and presented my case in the form of a table of carefully curated information. That bit of research saved us over a thousand dollars.

Besides the person, the writing is the main outcome of a PhD program. You could turn your dissertation into a book that will change the way people think – like my friend Lynne Kelly, who turned her PhD about indigenous oral knowledge-making practices into a popular book about Stonehenge. You could boil down the findings into your teaching and inspire your students. You can write articles and position papers, make documentaries or even museum exhibitions. You can design public health programs, a speaking tour, a festival ...

My point is, you've finished a PhD. You can turn that incredible creative energy and dedication to any number of projects if you want to. So next time you have an existential crisis, ask yourself these questions:

- Was my decision to start a PhD just inertia and now I've run out of puff? Or have I merely lost sight of my original motivations?
- What is my subconscious trying to tell me? Could I really be doing something more productive and interesting? If so, what does that look like?
- If the end point of my PhD is not academia, what are my other options? What do I need to do now to ensure that alternative career is a possibility?
- What's the best way for me to make a difference to the things I care about after I have finished my PhD?
- How am I different today than I was before? What have I learned about myself?

••• ACADEMIC ON THE INSIDE?

In December 2014, I was invited to give the keynote at the annual meeting of Australian postgraduate careers advisors in Sydney. Career counselling professionals with a special interest in PhD student issues are rare. Naturally, I leapt at the chance to spend a day with a whole group of professional PhD Job Whisperers.

In the afternoon, there was a panel discussion with three experienced HR consultants. These people hire PhD candidates into industries other than academia. It was a fascinating and, for me at least, an eye-opening discussion. The panel members told us how they worked with PhD graduates and what they thought of them. Since there weren't any PhD students in the room to offend, the panel was frank. Science graduates in particular were described as emotionally unaware, poor team players, bad communicators and inept project managers. The elastic deadlines in academia were criticised for breeding a culture of indifference to the value of time and a certain lack of pragmatism that doesn't work outside of academia.

It was hard to listen to the panel with a generous heart. Everything they were saying was contrary to what I observe in practice. I spend my working life helping

PhD students, the majority of whom are working in the sciences. I have enormous respect for the work scientists do. I admire their diligence, attention to detail, creativity and resilience. They tend to have strong communities and extended friendship networks because they often work in large teams. Contrary to many of the stereotypes in the media, scientists are ordinary people. Scientists can have pink hair, tattoos, T-shirts with incomprehensible slogans on them and hipster beards. The scientists I have come to know were not the 'propeller-head' stereotype being presented (yes, the panel actually used this term). OK, some of them are further along the autism spectrum than the majority of the population, but still.

At the end of the discussion, I felt I had to challenge the panel. In typical academic style, I went in at what I thought were the two weakest points in their argument: deadlines and teamwork. I started by pointing out that the pressure to get results and publish is intense in academia. Academics must manage ill-defined projects over long time frames. Academic work is often frustrating and needs a high degree of commitment, creativity and enthusiasm. Surely these are the right skills and attitudes for business?

Well, yes and no, apparently. The panel pointed out that, in business, decisions are often made on partial information. This can be uncomfortable for researchers who like to carefully collect evidence and do a considered analysis before offering an opinion. In fact, careful answers are what most academics hold dear; you are not an academic if you skip steps, leave out details or don't entertain the possibility you are wrong.

This so called 'communication problem' was beginning to look more like a culture clash to me. This feeling only intensified when I asked my next question. How was it possible, I asked the panel, for science graduates to be bad at teamwork? They grow up in a lab culture where sharing and collaborating are the norm. You can't really do science without collaborating at some level. After years and years of this, even those who are not naturally disposed to play well with others will surely pick up some team work skills.

Well yes, of course, the panellists replied. When you get a team of scientists working together in a non-academic setting, they collaborate like mad. They are the very model of best practice in teamwork. They just don't get along with *other* people that well – 'other people' being non-academics and people who are not trained in the same discipline. Scientists often found it difficult, the panellists explained, to communicate with non-scientists. Communication involves much more than merely translating technical terms and concepts into non-specialist speech. In the workplace, telling someone a fact is not enough; scientists have to learn to *use* the facts to persuade people to adopt a position or a new practice. Scientists do not usually have good skills in this because they are used to dealing with people who think the same way. This made sense to me – there are enough climate denial, anti-vaccination and anti-wind farm advocates out there, despite the best efforts of scientists to tell them the facts. Facts do not, in fact, speak for themselves.

If you do not get good at persuading people with facts, the communication problems multiply. The panellists gave examples of scientists criticising decisions they thought were wrong and asking uncomfortable questions they knew the other person couldn't answer. Basically, in fact, acting like normal academics. This kind of nitpicking, critical behaviour makes most non-academics feel stupid and defensive. It probably makes most academics feel the same way, to be honest, but we learn to hide it better. Combative academic behaviour that is perfectly acceptable in a lab meeting just makes you seem like, well, an asshole.

It seemed to me that the communication problems the panel members were describing are not easily solved. It's not that PhD students are not socialised properly – they are socialised too well. Everything about the PhD curriculum is designed to generate more academics, not researchers who work in business settings. If we do our jobs as educators, by the time they graduate most PhD students are very good academics, which means they are not likely to perform well in most business settings.

Changing this academic formula to produce more 'business-ready' graduates is dangerous. I don't just say that to resist change. We need criticism and extended timelines to make sure our research conclusions are as right as they can be. We wouldn't *be* academics if we didn't work this way – but we could work on being nicer to each other when applying this criticism. If you want to move outside of academia when you are finished – and 60 per cent of you will – you will need to be prepared for the possibility of culture shock. It probably won't be an easy transition, but does this mean you shouldn't do it?

I asked the panellists if any of the people they placed ever found the culture shock too much and went running back to academia. They claimed none of them did. Once accustomed to the new culture, most PhD graduates find non-academic settings quite comfortable. And they certainly like the pay!

💬 HOW TO MAKE ACADEMIC FRIENDS AND INFLUENCE PEOPLE

In a perfect world, research supervisors would not give preference to one student over another, but the world is far from perfect. Professors can and do have favourite students, which irritates the heck out of the students who realise they are not on the list. Being the favourite student is a form of power because it gives you additional access to a supervisor's time and resources. Working out how to become the favourite student can be difficult. I often meet new PhD students who are mystified by the subtle workings of academic pecking order, despite substantial career success in other industries. I always point the confused at Marian Petre and Gordon Rugg's *The Unwritten Rules of PhD Research*, an excellent book that contains a good discussion of instrumental and expressive behaviours.

Instrumental behaviours are goal-directed: things you do in order to get something done, or to find out things you need to know. Expressive behaviours demonstrate to others what kind of person you are. An example of an instrumental behaviour would be downloading articles that interest you and leaving it at that. The expressive behaviour counterpart would be to send articles you discover to others who might be interested in them. The expressive behaviour takes more effort because you have to be aware of the work of others around you. A genuine interest in people will help you here – unfortunately, it's a quality that can be in short supply in academia. Thinking about journal articles as tokens of academic affection is a whole other way to think about your work, but I would argue a useful and more pleasant way than being focussed solely on how your work will advance you or even the state of knowledge in the field.

No one will take the time to tell you, but your PhD years are also an introduction to the 'gift economy' in academia. The idea of a gift economy is a complex one, so I can only give it cursory treatment here. Basically the idea is that a gift performs a social function: it builds and cements relationships between people. Although a gift is given 'freely', there are a lot of unwritten rules about timing, expectations and reciprocity. For example, a gift should indicate the status of a relationship, particularly how reciprocal it is – which is why it can be embarrassing to get something really expensive from someone you hardly know.

Sharing a journal article is a kind of academic gift-giving that sends an important signal about you as a generous and interested academic. Sending a well-chosen, valuable, useful article at the right time is a lovely gesture, but it's important to realise that all gifts impose a obligation on the recipient. By sending an article you are (implicitly) imposing reading time on another person. Peppering your targets with journal articles is clumsy, and turns you from a generous colleague into an annoying one. Another form of academic gift-giving is donating time. Doing a guest lecture for a colleague is a nice way to donate time and expertise; reading over someone's draft is another.

Knowing how to use the right expressive behaviour at the right time is a form of insider knowledge. One could be paranoid and see this sort of insider knowledge as a form of power (which tends to be hoarded), or you could be more realistic and see the common failure to induct newbies into this knowledge as a sin of omission, rather than commission. Many academics will assume you know the things they know about academia, merely by virtue of the fact that you have had long experience as a student. But being a research student is very different from being an undergraduate. You are now a colleague-in-waiting and need to act like one in order to be taken seriously.

Writings on academic sociology – of which there is a surprising amount – are a great place to start finding out all the things that no one thinks to tell you. However, we at the Whisperer know you have a lot of reading to do on nuclear fusion, global terrorism and such like, so we try to do this sort of reading for you. Which is why I recently read with interest a book called *How Professors Think* by sociologist Michéle Lamont. The book is a fascinating and well-written account of how academics working on panels decide what grant proposals they will fund. One of the things the author was interested in was how academics come to recognise excellence – in academic work, but more importantly, how they decide if a colleague is excellent. Excellence in academia is a currency with which you 'buy' attention and respect. If your colleagues think you are excellent, you will have a lot more influence. So Lamont asked the panellists how they recognise a good peer review panellist. The answers revealed a hidden set of assumptions about what makes a good academic, which I think research students should heed.

The first thing mentioned was that a good panellist should show up fully prepared and ready to discuss the proposals. Those panellists who had carefully read the proposals – at least enough to be able to make thoughtful comments on them and argue their merits on the fly – were seen as most credible. Another desirable characteristic was the demonstration of intellectual breadth and expertise, which stemmed from the command of large literatures in their field and some adjacent ones. Along with this command of intellectual territory was the ability to be succinct and to respect other people's expertise and sentiments. After encountering more than a few pompous windbags, I have appreciation for academics who can make their point quickly and clearly, then move on. There are very few people who can intelligently comment on what they know while having the humbleness to be able to listen to and recognise people who have more expertise.

So there you have it: 'preparedness, expertise, succinctness, intellectual depth and multidisciplinary breadth and sensitivity to others', as Lamont puts it, are highly valued – among top humanities scholars sitting on these peer review panels, at least. I wouldn't be surprised if these qualities translate more generally and into the sciences; I hope similar research is done to see if this is indeed the case. I suspect carefully cultivating these qualities and learning how to display them through appropriate expressive behaviour is the work of a lifetime, which is probably why many of the best of us are also the oldest.

I often read advice to new colleagues which basically boils down to 'If you want to get ahead, be selfish'. I think this advice is wrong-headed because it completely denies the existence and value of the Academic Gift Culture. If you pay time into your network, you will be rewarded – though perhaps not in the way you expect. Blogging is a good example. I blog because I find it an intrinsically enjoyable activity. I like to write, but

I don't like writing 'academese'. Blogging is a creative outlet, but the blog posts act as gifts and people reciprocate all the time, often in delightfully unexpected ways. As my friend Kate Gemmell puts it, you have to earn the right to ask a favour.

However, I have to temper this enthusiasm with a note of caution: the gift economy is precious and always under threat, especially in the contemporary 'metricised' academy. Thomas Hylland Eriksen wrote what is perhaps the definitive article on the academic gift economy. In it he points out that if your gifts are motivated by shallow opportunism they will not work to make your network stronger. Eriksen then points out the fragility of this culture, where the free time we have to offer others is threatened by draconian work plans that limit the number of hours that can be spent on gifting:

> Much of the disillusion and unhappiness in today's
> universities is caused by the fact that their academic
> employees are about to be deprived of the right
> to spend a fair proportion of their working hours
> doing free work for others. A good academic
> publishes both nationally and internationally. It may
> indeed often seem as if books and articles published
> are all that counts. However, those of us who work
> inside the system know otherwise. It is gratifying
> to have one's work published wherever one likes,

but the publications are part of a larger ecology kept going by a very substantial amount of largely unrecognized work. Those who publish without contributing to this invisible ecology may rightly be considered freeriders.[*]

Eriksen points out that if achievement is all that counts in hiring processes, and gifting is ignored, we suffer a range of unintended consequences. Certainly academic assholes thrive in such a miserable atmosphere. This is why I cling tightly to my academic gifting practices – sometimes at the expense of working long hours, it must be said. I am lucky, at the moment, to work in a place that puts a premium on the academic gift culture. Personally, I plan to make this a prerequisite for any future employment situation. What kind of academic do you want to be – generous or a miser? It's a choice only you can make, but I know my answer.

---

[*]   'Farewell to the academic gift economy?', 9 July 2006, <hyllanderiksen.net/Gifteconomy.html>.

ON THE IMPORTANCE OF BEING INTERESTING

One of the hardest parts of my job at ANU is the Three Minute Thesis competition (3MT). The 3MT is an international competition for PhD students with a few simple rules. You must tell a non-academic audience what your research is about, how you are doing it and why anyone should care – in just three minutes. Just to make it harder, you are only allowed one slide as a presentation aid, and no animations, transitions, sounds, costumes or musical instruments (just in case you were wondering).

In theory, it shouldn't be difficult to persuade research candidates to participate in this competition, if only for the prize money, but in practice it's very hard to get people to engage. My team and I spend six months of the year marketing the hell out of this competition. We pepper PhD candidates and their supervisors with messages selling the many benefits of participating. We prepare a special training series with specialists such as speechwriters and performance coaches to help them hone a perfect script. We even hire a graphic designer to help them make that one perfect slide. But, despite our best efforts, the vast majority of PhD students at ANU don't take up the challenge.

I understand the reluctance to participate, I really do. Brevity is hard. Blaise Pascal (or so the story goes) once wrote to a friend: 'I would have written a shorter letter, but I did not have the time.' But I don't believe it's the difficulty that really puts our PhD students off. They are doing a PhD, after all. I think the reasons are more about culture; in particular, attitudes towards competition. Academia is a highly competitive profession, but we don't like to mention it out loud. The contest of ideas is not meant to have a winner. A winner-takes-all contest belongs in sport, not academia (and most of us are academics because we weren't very good at sports). The stated aim of the 3MT is to 'sell' research to the general public. The emphasis here is on the sizzle, not the sausage. This emphasis on the form of the communication, not its content, can be viewed as a little bit unsavoury in a culture in pursuit of knowledge and truth.

I'm indebted to Annie McCarthy, at the time a PhD student at ANU, for a better understanding of the PhD student attitude to the 3MT. On Facebook Annie wrote about how the 3MT is positioned as something only for newbie scholars:

> Every time I hear a senior academic speak about
> the competition they all say something like 'I could
> never talk about my research in three minutes'.
> Which begs the question 'why the hell not?' and the

secondary question of 'is that because it's actually impossible?' And if that's the case, what kind of dichotomy is the three minute thesis setting up, on the one hand confining senior academics to the land of waffling obscurity and young graduate students to the fast lane of the commercially viable drive through takeaway.

Woman has a point – why is it only 'junior' academics that are seen to be in need of this kind of training and experience? A successful career as a researcher depends on more than just smarts. You have to be able to sell yourself and your research to others, and that includes other academics. And this is where I have a slight problem with the 3MT as a concept.

Three minutes is too long.

Yes, you heard me right. Most people won't give you three minutes to explain anything unless you are up on a stage and they are in the audience. Most times you have three sentences to explain yourself to anyone, even in academia. Consider the academic conference or seminar tea table. The common conversational opener 'What is your research about?' is an invitation to academic small talk, not an invitation to give a mini-lecture, as some people seem to assume. It's vitally important that you have a killer opening sentence in answer to this question. In lieu of a lecture you need an opening 'bit' that makes people want to talk to you more. Talking builds connections, and connections build careers. You need one sentence intriguing enough to help the rest of the conversation unfold. More importantly, it needs to be easy to remember.

My PhD research was about how hand gestures are used by teachers and students in architecture classrooms, but that didn't sound very interesting. My one-sentence opener was: 'I'm studying how architects talk with their hands'. Often I just left it at that – if people are curious they will ask questions, which they almost inevitably did. At the moment, I am part of a team doing a project in machine learning, developing natural language processing algorithms. My new one-sentence opener is: 'We're trying to teach machines how to read job advertisements.' This one-liner is a bit of a deliberate tease. I'm not really trying to explain what I'm doing, but to give people an easy opening to ask questions if they want to. It's also meant to make people think I am an interesting person doing interesting research.

Being interesting is an important, but little recognised, cultural asset for a researcher. One of the best pieces of advice I ever got about communications is that people will not remember what you say, but they will remember how you made them feel. Academic small talk is a chance to make people feel they just met someone interesting. I think the 3MT is a perfect training ground to develop that vital skill of being interesting, but I know that next year I'm still going to have to work hard to convince yet another generation of PhD students this is the case – such is my lot in life!

IF YOU BLOG, WILL YOU LOSE YOUR JOB?

This post was one of a shitstorm of online protests about La Trobe University's suspension of an academic because she was outed as a Marxist on social media. I was in Canada when I saw the story break, very early, in Australia. I was able to write and post this, out of my usual schedule, in time for my 30 000-odd subscribers to read it before they had breakfast. Some ten hours after this was posted, largely in response to a couple of online petitions and the negative commentary on the hashtag #istandwithrozward, La Trobe University backed down and reinstated the academic.

The Thesis Whisperer is truly a labour of love. It does not fit in my work week, which is filled to the brim with meetings, teaching and other commitments. I edit contributions and write my own posts on the weekend, mostly on quiet Sunday afternoons when my boys are amusing themselves with video games, bike riding or some other activity they like to do together. It takes about ten hours a month, depending on how creative I feel. I love curling up with a cup of tea and my laptop on the couch to read guest contributions, edit, write correspondence and new posts. I don't want to uncritically promote the culture of overwork in the academy, but if I didn't do my blog work on the weekend it just wouldn't happen. I honestly enjoy this time spent in what I consider a form of public service. I know people appreciate this work and I feel a deep sense of pleasure every time someone tells me that they value the blog. I tell them that it runs on love and they have just added fuel to the love fire, but I'd be lying if I didn't say there was a selfish side.

The blog is of enormous value to my career. I'm relatively senior now and must still do all those things an associate professor needs to do: teach, research and manage other people. But the blog means I get noticed. Sometimes the people I get noticed by are in a position to offer me things: jobs, travel, publishing deals, information and advice. I could have published in academic journals forever and never enjoyed such benefits from my writing. My high profile means I am often asked to talk about my work on social media in public forums. There is always at least one question from the audience along the lines of 'Will blogging put my job at risk?' If the forum is for students, the question will be something like 'Will blogging mean no one will want to hire me?' I used to dismiss these concerns out of hand, but now I don't. I talk about blogging with great fondness and enthusiasm, but I stop short of suggesting to others that they should do it. In fact, over the years I have become more and more cautious in the advice I give, despite the clear advantages I have enjoyed. My public engagement online has always been positive, but this is not so for other academics, and sometimes the blame for this can be laid directly at the feet of their university.

This morning, I read yet another article about an academic being suspended from their job because of a perfect internet storm – in this case, the combination of highly public and controversial work, sexism, personal politics, homophobia and a breach of online privacy. Rather than try to explain it, I'm going to quote at length from the Campus Morning Mail, the indispensable gossip sheet information digest that Stephen Matchett compiles and circulates by email to academics all over Australia.

Stephen does a good job of outlining what has happened in this case.

La Trobe University has charged Roz Ward with serious misconduct and suspended her employment.

Ms Ward was an advisor to the Victorian state government's taskforce on bullying of LGBTI students in schools but resigned after a Facebook post in which she suggested a red flag should fly over state parliament instead of the 'racist Australian one.' University HR director Fiona Reed stood Ms Ward down yesterday. La Trobe was not commenting last night saying it was following normal HR process. The university has previously expressed concern at the impact of Ms Ward's comment on the credibility of La Trobe researchers in her field. However the National Tertiary Education Union, which is advising Ms Ward, isn't having any of it. 'The media attack on Roz Ward, purportedly about a social media post about the Australian flag, is in reality part of a concerted political and ideological campaign by Australia's right wing ideologues on views that do not accord with their own,' NTEU Victorian Secretary, Dr Colin Long said last night. 'The hysterical response to Ms Ward's private Facebook posting about the Australian flag is typical of the right's absolute refusal to consider the ways in which racism is expressed, often unconsciously, in symbols, institutions and attitudes. That La Trobe University has apparently allowed itself to be cowed into participating in this anti-intellectual, anti-democratic attack reflects the dismal state of intellectual capacity at the senior management level in some Australian universities.' *

Whatever you think of Ms Ward's politics, I'd hope you would agree she has the right to have her Marxist opinions. She also has the presumed right to post on a closed Facebook account in peace. A 'friend' leaking what she said about the Australian flag to the mainstream media is something she probably didn't expect to happen and hearing about it sends a chill down my spine. It's one of the great pleasures of my life that my Facebook feed is full of academics, because they are full of opinions and happy to share them – and I'm no different. We are especially opinionated about politics. Oh, how we love to spout off our critical discourse theory take on Tony Abbott eating an onion, or deconstruct Peter Dutton's fruitless attempts to stop becoming an internet meme. Many of us share our outrage about our current government's stance on issues like refugees and marriage equality. Academics are highly intelligent, and often very witty – especially when they are angry. My world would be a poorer place without this online

* *Campus Morning Mail*, 2 June 2016, <campusmorningmail.com.au/aspirational-atar-alternative>.

banter, which, frankly, helps me cope with my own sadness and anger.

Although I don't identify as Marxist, I totally understand Roz Ward's jokey moment with a friend. How terrible for her that it snowballed out of control and how shameful that her university not only failed to support her, but piled on with the other attackers. Regrettably, this is not the first time an academic has found that their university has no stomach for defending them against attacks by the mainstream media. Let's compare what happened to Dr Ward with the attack by right-wing columnist Andrew Bolt on Martin Hirst – who happens to be another Marxist. Dr Hirst was saved through a petition by his academic colleagues. I'm not going to publicly comment about the role of the News Corp paper *The Australian* in that matter, for fear of being sued or attacked myself. And this is precisely the problem. ANU has been unfailingly supportive of my online activities. I don't want to put them in the centre of a mainstream media shitstorm – so I censor myself. But can I censor everyone else as well? As one of my academic friends, Deb Verhoeven, said on Facebook this morning:

> It's another layer of self monitoring. It reminds
> me of the way people are taught 'defensive driving'
> – you have to assume everyone around you is a

potential danger. So you are no longer responsible
for your own actions on the academic superhighway
but the actions of everybody else as well.

Deb is right. Over dinner you can say what you like
about *The Australian* with your academic friends. Unless
you are being recorded, you always have plausible deni-
ability. However, if you say the same thing online, you
might find yourself in trouble with your employer. Anything digital can escape its context – this is both its
great strength and its great danger. Email is perhaps the
most dangerous form of digital communication of all.
An email feels very private, but it can be shared with a
mainstream outlet like *The Australian* with the simple
click of a mouse.

So if you are an academic, should you blog or otherwise be present and opinionated online?

Well, it depends. If you do fairly uncontroversial
student support work like myself, it's probably fine and
blogging can be the source of pleasure and advantage
it has been for me. I should note that I am careful to
avoid putting too many images of myself in association
with the Whisperer, for fear of attracting the Sad Puppy
types who hate women having any kind of public voice.
If you have a highly political or controversial research
domain you might, one day, find yourself hung out to
dry by university management. I don't blog on religion,

climate change, racism or politics because it's not my area. I'd like to think if I was a scholar of those topics I would, but in my heart I know I wouldn't. I just don't have the guts, resilience and determination to do so.

What I can do, however, is support academics who blog on controversial and risky topics, even if I don't agree with everything they write – and so should their university. I want these academics to be able to curl up with a cup of tea on the couch and do their blogging work with pleasure, just like I do. I've done work for La Trobe University in the past, but I certainly won't again if there is not some sensible resolution to this issue. La Trobe University management needs to show leadership and give its academics confidence that they can have opinions – which, after all, is what we are paid to do.

#istandwithRozWard

NICHE MARKETING FOR ACADEMICS

An article in the *Guardian* titled 'I'm a serious academic, not a professional instagrammer' caused a bit of a stir in my online community. The basic thrust of the piece was that those who engage in social media are just showing off. Tseen Khoo on *The Research Whisperer* blog pointed out that the author was indulging in a bit of humble-bragging and Sophie Lewis responded with a nice piece called Blogging While Academic, so there doesn't seem to be much more to add. However, the article, and the reactions to it, did get me thinking (again) about the discomfort many academics feel with the idea of self-promotion.

There's a lot of bitching about social media, but that's just a distraction – the academic game hasn't really changed. Academia has always been a noisy marketplace of ideas. Getting people to pay attention to you and your work is a necessary part of finding that next job, building collaborations, landing that next grant, and so on. If social media helps, I say use it.

Let's take publishing and that nebulous idea of 'impact' as a concrete example of the academic ideas marketplace in action. Governments around the world are obsessed with making sure they get value for money from academics. They have a range of measures to check whether we are disseminating the research they pay for. These measures translate from the government, via your department, as a pressure to publish. But with the rise of the so-called 'impact agenda', the message is no longer 'Publish or perish' but, as my friend John Lamp puts it, 'Be visible or vanish'.

One of the easiest ways to measure academic impact is through citations (how many people mention your paper in their paper). There are a lot of valid arguments about citations being a bad form of measurement, but where there is a number it will be used. The working academic can't afford to completely ignore citation measures if they are interested in getting a new job or a promotion. I try not to focus on the numbers: my strategy is to focus on the most urgent, difficult-to-solve problems in my field (at the moment it's PhD graduate employability). I've found that attempting to solve these problems is intrinsically interesting. When you do research on the truly important problems there is always a potential audience of people in your field who want to read your work. Generally, people will be grateful if you make it easy for them to find it. Really, your problem is not so much self-promotion, as communicating with your niche audience that you have something new to share.

Let's face it, most academics are pretty bad at this kind of 'niche marketing'. Evidence shows that many published papers are not widely read and a startlingly large number of articles are never cited. In my popular workshop 'Write That Journal Article in 7 Days', I make the point that getting through the peer review process is not the end of the publishing adventure, but a mid-point where the writing finishes and the promoting begins. At the end of the workshop, I offer a few easy niche marketing communication strategies – here are a few of them.

Email your finished paper to a couple of people on your reference list

The people you cite are the people most likely to be interested in how their research has been used. Your list of references is bound to contain a few notables in your field. Summon up your courage, write a nice cover letter (with an appropriate fangirl/fanboy greeting) and press send. I've done this a few times in the past and never had to wait more than about 24 hours for a response. The person is usually humbly pleased that you have read their work and interested in what you have to share. You never know – they might even cite it in their next paper and give you an 'uplift'. Or they might ask you if you are going to be visiting their town or attending the next big conference in the field. Write back and make a date for coffee.

Networking?
Handled.

Share it on Twitter

Obviously social media is only an effective promotion channel if you have spent some time building a network of followers. I could bore for Australia on social media tactics, but I only have space here for one top tip. Hunt for people or hashtags in your area of research and include these in your tweets. #phdchat is an amazing resource to help you find the people and hashtags you are interested in. Craft a polite tweet asking people on #phdchat for help and you will be surprised by the deluge of helpful information that can result. What about ResearchGate and academia.edu, I hear you asking? Well, it's complicated. I'll have to save that question for another time.

Work the specialist email lists

There's an email list in my area that is quite difficult to get added to, but when you are finally shown the secret handshake ... oh my! Everyone who is anyone in the field of research education is on that list. It took me three years to get someone to recommend me to be accepted, but now I have a connection to just about everyone in the world who does research on research education. Sometimes the old-fashioned ways are the best. People use that list to share what they have been writing. I compose most of my new reading list from this feed. Ask colleagues what lists they are on and how they got access. There's likely to be a whole network just below your feet. But be careful. Each list has unwritten rules about how to behave. You don't want to crash the party by posting too often, or about the 'wrong' things. Lurk. Spend at least a couple of months observing how people behave before posting.

———

Inevitably, when I finish presenting my full list of strategies I am looking into a room full of shell-shocked students. Many candidates have been so focussed on getting that paper written they haven't stopped to think about the next step.

I get a variety of responses to these suggestions, some of which boil down to 'Do I really have to do this?! I'm an academic, not a PR professional!' Some of my colleagues get genuinely upset by my enthusiastic approach to academic niche marketing. I get the feeling they think self-promotion is quite unseemly, but successful academics have always promoted their work. If you have something good to share, I see no problem with any of what I suggested above. Self-promotion, when your 'product' is good and something people want, is not odious, pushy or obnoxious – it's just extra work.

Do the work. You won't regret it.

💬 #FIFOACADEMIC

Australia is a big country. You can fit almost the whole of the UK into Victoria, our second-smallest state. The folks at ANU were happy to let me commute the 512 kilometres between Canberra and Melbourne while Thesis Whisperer Jnr finished primary school. I flew in halfway through Monday and flew out halfway through Thursday. I had a small bedsit on campus in one of the residential colleges. What an interesting experience it was, too... maybe one day I'll write a Jane Goodall–style book called *Living Among the Undergraduates*. Anyway, Australia is a huge, sparsely populated country, so there are many 'fly-in fly-out' (FIFO) workers. Most of them work in the mining industry, but a surprising number of people in academia FIFO too.

I was lucky to spend the first 15 years of my academic career in one city. If you stay in academia long enough, it's highly likely you will have to move to get the job you want. The most common reason people choose to commute is called the 'two body problem' which *Slate* describes as:

> an inelegant term for the difficulty that couples have in finding good jobs for both people that are geographically close enough that they can continue to live together. Given the shortage of full-time academic jobs, couples are frequently put in a position where they have to choose between serious underemployment for one of them and living separately.*

When talking to younger colleagues about career choices I encourage them to think about their own emotional, financial and intellectual needs in relation to the uncertainties of a long-term academic career. There are many complex factors to consider. In the 'post-post-postdoc' stage of an academic career, where short-term contracts are the norm, some people are forced to move a lot – maybe even once or twice a year. This 'hyper-mobility' has personal consequences, especially for women. Compared to men, women have a relatively short time frame to decide whether or not to procreate. You hear stories of women having kids at 60, but I know

---

* Matt Reed, 'Two bodies, one job', *Slate*, 3 October 2013.

from first-hand experience that you can be infertile much younger than that. Academic hyper-mobility makes the procreation decision, which is always tricky, even more fraught. Many people decide to have kids on their own, but most of us do it in pairs. I know of a few married academics who happily live with oceans between them, but it wouldn't work for me. I like having my husband around and couldn't bear being separated from my child for too long. However, my work is highly specialised, which means my options are necessarily limited. Finding a situation where home and work needs were balanced took a long time. I have achieved it, but not by being 'strategic'. I just said 'yes' to opportunities that seemed likely to move me closer to the happy balance of work and home I had in mind.

Making choices about where to live and work can be difficult, especially at the start of your career. You might not even realise a choice is a mistake until years later. Sometimes choices don't feel like choices, either. Unless you are independently wealthy, your only 'choice' is to take the option that says 'money'. When you have a family, the decision about where to live is not just about you, which makes the whole process even more confusing. Fortunately for me, Mr Thesis Whisperer turned out to be very portable. I want to highlight that this is because he's not an academic. If you hook up with another academic, the complexity of the mobility problem can become unbearable. However, moving Thesis Whisperer Jnr was another matter altogether. Some children can be moved from one country to another without batting an eyelid, but Thesis Whisperer Jnr is not one of those children. The year of living FIFO let him move schools at a natural point between primary school and high school and I had a year to find exactly the right school for him, which turned out very well.

If you are a woman, you need to listen to advice from straight, white men with a critical ear. To be clear, straight white men are often not being deliberately sexist – they just experience academia very differently. They might fail to realise that what is good advice for other men might not be good advice for women with aspirations to have children. In heteronormative academic-to-academic relationships, the woman is far more likely to become the 'trailing spouse', following the man from city to city. This happens because the couple make pragmatic choices.

Let me explain how this happens with a true story. A woman in a postdoc position decides to take a year off to have a baby between jobs. So far, so normal. However, when she tries to get back into the workforce, despite all those words about 'relative to opportunity' in the job ads, she's not getting interviews. There's a hole in her CV where papers should be and it's getting bigger all the time. She tells me how all the knock-backs are making her feel disheartened, so she decides she might as well have another kid. The childcare costs are crippling and the casual hours are difficult to manage, so she gives up working as a part-time lecturer. Meanwhile, her husband has been publishing his butt off and, as a result, gets offered a postdoc position in another city. Of course, they move. It seems like a mutual decision, but really it's the structure of the academic workforce and its demand for mobility that's forcing their hand. It's the pragmatic choice to take the sure thing – children must be fed.

Fast forward a couple of years. He's working late and travelling more as he climbs the academic ladder. She's doing a lot of (unpaid and unrecognised) work to get her family settled in a new city, but it's going well. They have a nice house in the good school district. We have lunch when I happen to be in town and she tells me about the publishing she's doing now the kids are in school and she can do some teaching on the side. Things are starting to look up for her, but the very next week she calls me, delighted. They are moving to another country! This is a great opportunity for him/them. Finally a permanent role! No more fearful wait for the next job. This permanent job will help pay for the insane mortgage that enables the children to attend the 'good' school in the 'right' suburb. I murmur supportive things, but in my heart I suspect it's the end of her academic dreams.

As it turns out, I was right. She has now fully accepted and embraced the role of trailing spouse. She has lost the networks of patronage so essential to working at the margins of academia. She takes up a non-academic job in her husband's new university. The primary attraction of this role is the flexible hours so she can attend to the children's needs and build their lives in a new country. On Skype she tells me how she misses the research, but she feels like she is part of something again, you know? Being in a team is much better than watching from the sidelines. I can certainly understand this. I did 11 years as a casual academic. I well remember the feeling of being on the academic margins. You can start to feel like you're looking in the window of a happy house at Christmas time. Good news, though – her daughter is doing well at school. Apparently little Anna wants to be a scientist. Maybe she'll have a better chance of making it work?

Actually that story is not strictly true, it's kind of 'truthy'. It's the career/life story arc of at least six of my female friends, mixed together to make sense as a single story. Ask around. Variations of this story are everywhere with different degrees of happiness and unhappiness. There are precious few stories of people making the two body problem work, and I wish we had more. So think about the academic life as coming hand-in-hand with the need to be mobile. How can you make it work for you?

6

BEING POLITICAL

This last chapter is a collection of columns I have written for the National Tertiary Education Union (NTEU) newsletter. I was passed this rather delightful gig by a colleague and thoroughly enjoy the opportunity to get my rant on once every couple of months. They even pay me!

The best part of the union rag gig is being able to comment on current events as they occur. #distractinglysexy was a brief but entertaining internet meme that developed when a Nobel Prize winner made some really unfortunate comments about women in a very public forum. The Addiction contains some thoughts about the problem of sessional teaching, and resulted in a flurry of letters from members of the #auscasuals faction of the union. These are people caught in the casual teaching trap. More than one person has told me this column caused them to reconsider their whole career and decide to stop giving the university free labour. In

We Don't Measure Enough I talk about my frustration with the crude forms of metrics that are often imposed on academics as a way to 'improve performance'. Rather than complaining about the existence of metrics, I talk about how forms of accountability have to be carefully designed to work properly. More often than not, these metrics are limited by the skills of the people tasked with doing the design work. #democracysausage contrasts the attitude of our Australian politicians to those in other countries in Asia and looks at our lack of ambition for the higher education sector generally. In Fake Nostalgia I reflect on watching the grief of the baby boomer generation for a type of academic life that I, and many of my colleagues, have never been privileged enough to experience. In The Angry Rant Reconsidered I try to focus on the positive for a change, but maybe I didn't really succeed … Finally, and very appropriately I think, I include my thanks to the former Prime Minister Gough Whitlam. Without Gough, this book would not have been possible.

💬 #DISTRACTINGLYSEXY

For those of you who missed it, social media exploded when the famous Nobel Prize–winning scientist Professor Tim Hunt did the verbal equivalent of shooting himself in the foot (or was it the head?) at the World Conference of Science Journalists. Hunt, who apparently has a reputation for being 'a bit of a chauvinist', spoke in favour of single-sex labs by telling the audience of JOURNALISTS that 'three things happen when they [women] are in the lab ... You fall in love with them, they fall in love with you and when you criticise them, they cry.'

Apparently his speech was greeted with polite applause in Korea, where the conference was being held. Not so on Twitter, where the outrage was immediate and the mocking had begun before he had even left the podium. Female scientists started posting pictures of themselves in all kinds of unglamorous outfits and situations, with the hashtag #distractinglysexy. The photos reflected the everyday life of a working scientist, of any gender, and perfectly demonstrated the folly of Hunt's remarks. Some women posted pictures of themselves hugging machines which they claim to have fallen in love with, or posted safety diagrams warning men that lady tears might be a slip hazard.

What happened next was interesting.

I thought the relevant institutions would have to be shamed into taking action, but Hunt was swiftly asked to resign from prestigious positions at both the University College London and the Royal Society. You can't help but wonder if his 'reputation as a bit of chauvinist' was coming back to haunt him. In my experience, management can be well aware of the bigots inside their operation, but often lack the grounds to take action. People who are victimised tend to remain silent for fear of retribution. Everything changes in the full glare of the media spotlight. Justice, however much delayed, can be swift and terrible.

Apparently Hunt was dismayed and bewildered by the shitstorm he created. Perhaps if he'd encountered enough outright rebuffs to his casually sexist comments over the years, things might have been different the other day in Korea. But I'm not surprised, really. People are usually polite, especially to Nobel Prize–winners, and it's hard to speak back to power.

Actually – it can be hard to speak back to sexism. Full stop.

Just the other week I was running a workshop where a couple of men in the 55-and-over age bracket made a series of sexually charged 'jokes' in response to an exercise. There was uneasy, embarrassed laughter from the class. I realised everyone was looking to me for guidance, but I just froze. I didn't know what to do.

Why?

Inside, I felt like I was ten years old again, feeling outraged by a boy snapping my bra strap, then calling me ugly when I told him to stop.

I was 13 again, listening to the boys behind me cataloguing who was hot and who wasn't and enduring the mocking laughter when I asked them to stop.

I was 16 again, mentally preparing myself to be verbally harassed by random men when I got on a train, or walked past a building site, or just basically existed in a public space.

I was 20 again, listening to men at a party tell sexist jokes. 'What's wrong? Don't you have a sense of humour?' they asked when I didn't laugh right away. 'You know that no one wants to screw a feminist, right?'

Over the years, many men have policed my behaviour, probably without realising it. All these years in a female body taught me to say nothing, to back down, to avoid the fight. I've learned not to call out sexist behaviour, or draw too much attention to myself. It's hardly surprising that when I was faced with being mocked by a group of men in the classroom, I effectively did nothing. By that I mean I did what so many women probably did when Hunt was developing his reputation as a bit of a chauvinist: I kept the peace by laughing it off. I changed the subject. I pretended it didn't happen. Then

I felt self-loathing at the betrayal of my feminist ideals. You can't win!

I would love to say that from now on I will always speak back, but it will happen again. I know many men worry that the workplace is becoming a 'politically correct' minefield. Maybe it is – but that's only because change is hard for everyone. Listening and asking questions is the first step. All men should listen carefully to the laughter of women. Does it come from the belly, or is it just polite? Does the woman look embarrassed and change the subject?

It's hard, yes – but in a way it's also easy. If you're worried you've caused offence, just ask: 'Was what I said ok?' If it wasn't, apologise. Try to avoid saying it again. There's no need to become a hashtag.

💬 THE ADDICTION

I have a friend, let's call her Helen.

Helen recently completed a PhD and is now in the post-post-postdoc stage of the academic wilderness. Helen is not a scientist, so her academic life now consists entirely of three-month sessional contracts and guest lectures (most of which are unpaid). If you have done this for any stretch of time you will know it's not a great way to make a living. The November to February non-teaching months are particularly hard. Just when everyone else is out shopping, your wallet is empty.

Helen rang me to tell me how, as usual, Christmas had precipitated a financial crisis. She sobbed as she told me how behind she was on the rent and that she could barely afford the other necessities of life. She told me she looked to me as a role model of a successful academic, because I did 11 years as a sessional.

What should she do to be more like me?

It's not the first time I've taken this call from a friend doing sessional teaching. People in Helen's situation want to know how I made the seemingly impossible leap from tenuous periphery to associate professor at a prestigious research university.

Getting a proper job, one that enables you to start climbing the academic ladder, is a bit like trying to get inside a moving car with three locked doors. Sessional teachers who want a 'proper job' often find themselves in a vicious, chicken-and-egg situation. You can apply for everything that you are qualified for and still not be shortlisted because of the premium Australian employers put on experience. You can be a great researcher, but this doesn't count as much as already having had a job as a researcher – and these jobs are certainly in short supply. Unless you get a lucky break, you might never be in a job that lets you evidence skills you already have, so you will never be truly competitive.

This, as you can imagine, can make you feel powerless. People like Helen want to take action. The assumption these people make about my story is that it was something I did that made me different. They want to do something too. What they fail to take into account is that academia is now structured with very few entry points and some people start closer to the finish line. They are inevitably disappointed with my advice. Yes, blogging is a really good idea – if you like it, and you can do it. Yes, building networks is essential for any professional career. Yes, developing a clear and useful specialty, like research education, is helpful.

But I had to tell Helen the truth. The difference between her and me was ... a husband.

Yes, my secret career weapon is Luke, my beloved spouse and well-paid computer scientist. For nearly

20 years now Luke's 'unstable' private sector job has counterbalanced my 'stable' public sector one. Luke's income meant that Christmas never caused a crisis in our household. Crucially, Luke supported my long periods of study and had faith that it would all pay off eventually.

Helen quickly ruled out the husband option, so we started casting about for other solutions. 'What is the adjacent possible?' I asked. Could Helen get a job in a university with many of the features that she enjoyed without the perilous paycheck situation?

Helen hesitated.

'It's like this, Inger ... I love teaching,' she confessed, almost shamefully. 'I love to see the light come on in their eyes.'

My heart sank.

Helen, like so many, many other people I know, is addicted to teaching.

The addicted sessional teacher is willing to endure the low pay, uncertainty and knock-backs because they are hooked on that classroom experience. This teaching addiction explains why there is such a ready supply of people willing to do casual sessional work, when it clearly doesn't pay the bills. I know exactly how this addiction feels because I was once addicted too. In fact, I probably still am, but, ironically, the more stable my employment becomes the less classroom time I have.

Our sector needs to take responsibility and recognise its role as an enabler. Teaching addiction is real and it is severely affecting the wellbeing of Helen and many like her. Yes, teaching is fun. It makes you feel like you're making a difference. But universities should not implicitly rely on teaching addiction to make sure there is a ready and able workforce.

It's literally wrecking lives.

Gently I told Helen I thought it was time to stop. I told her she deserved better from her employers. That she should be valued and paid a decent living wage for her labour. But, like many addicts, she just didn't want to hear.

She hung up on me.

WE DON'T MEASURE ENOUGH

The problem with universities is not that we measure things like student satisfaction and research output, but that we don't measure enough.

Do I have your attention yet? I thought so. Measurement has become something of a touchy issue in academic circles. That opening statement probably made some of you angry, but let me explain before you jump to your keyboards to flame the NTEU for giving me a column to air my views.

Performance metrics – generating data about how well or badly the university performs on various activities – has become something of an obsession for governments of right- and left-wing persuasions. Universities have whole units of people dedicated to monitoring performance and reporting back to government. Despite cries from academics that measuring student feedback is not a way to ensure quality teaching, or that counting research publications is no way to ensure research quality, there's no sign of this trend ending any time soon.

The complaints are justified: measurement can produce perverse effects. Let's take research metrics as an example. Universities count the number of papers published, the number of research students graduated and the amount of competitive grant money won and deem an academic 'research active', or not. Recently my institution started enforcing standards laid out in the Higher Education Standards Framework (HESF), which was quietly passed into law in 2011. Non-research active academics cannot be a primary supervisor for a research student, who must be stewarded by another staff member.

Research supervision quality problems solved?

Well, not really.

This measure of research activity is as much a measure of privilege as it is of performance or ability. When achievements are seen as the work of the (heroic) individual, other aspects of the research environment which contribute to this success are wiped away. Access to research leave, access to new students, access to grant money is difficult for some researchers, particularly early-career researchers. But it is not only the privilege argument that can be mounted against the use of such crude measures, there is also a quality argument. No university, to my knowledge, counts the 'churn' of a supervisor – the number of students he or she loses in the process – in the measure of research activity.

Dumping underperforming research students – often women and minorities who have more trouble negotiating the academic environment – is a sensible, if heartless, strategy for supervisors who have a weather eye to their performance indicators. In my work as a research educator I have seen countless examples of this practice in action, even more so since I started blogging and hearing research student stories from around the world. Churn represents a huge cost in human misery and money, and its effects are often hidden from direct view. In many institutions you will find people who clean up the mess. Some of these people are the so-called 'angel supervisors' – academics who are experienced in helping research students who have fallen by the wayside. Others are early-career researchers, who cut their research supervising teeth through picking up the leftover students. In many cases the clean-up crew are not formally recognised for this work, or their record looks poor because they are primarily dealing with students who are at risk of not finishing at all.

You might be thinking something like 'Not everything that counts can be measured' – but, these days, most of it can. Universities continue to use extremely crude techniques to measure performance when much more supple and powerful ones are available. My tiny 11-inch Mac-Book Air, smaller than an A4 piece of paper, can perform incredible feats of number-crunching. I have been using it to dabble in the emerging field of social network analysis, which concentrates on the connections, rather than the individuals. It seems to me that there is vast, untapped potential in this form of analysis. If we start measuring research performance differently, treating the basic unit of measurement as clusters rather than individuals, the strategies we can use to increase output (and happiness) increase too. We can stop concentrating our efforts on blaming and remediating 'poor performers' and start looking at the conditions that cause poor performance to exist in the first place.

So why aren't we doing it? The answer, I suspect, is that counting individuals is easier and cheaper. You don't need particularly highly trained staff to manage spreadsheets, whereas social network analysis requires people like myself: researchers who are critically informed and can ask the right questions. We deserve better measuring from our employers, so let's stop fighting performance measures and start demanding *better* measurement practices – one indicator at a time.

💬 #DEMOCRACYSAUSAGE

Compulsory voting is one of the best things about our country. I love all the rituals: choosing a polling booth by the quality of the sausage sizzle; walking along the 'how to vote' card handout line while loftily ignoring all the parties one doesn't intend to vote for; getting a goodie or two at the cake stall. It's a tradition our nation can truly feel proud of – there is even a hashtag #democracysausage so people can share their election day culinary experiences. Our family usually caps the day off by watching the results coming in on the ABC with friends and exclaiming, 'Oh, that Antony Green, such a clever clogs!'.

It's all great fun.

Except for this year.[*]

Being of a generally left-wing persuasion, the group that gathered at my sister's house on Saturday night found little comfort in these rituals. Julia Gillard, Australia's first female prime minister, was gone. Bitter comments were muttered in the general direction of the television and even Antony didn't cheer us up. For my part there was a certain amount of self-soothing with chocolate. When the inevitable result was announced

---

[*] 2013

I did a one-word Facebook status update and went straight to bed. A couple of weeks later it all seems to have gone quiet in Canberra. Maybe those politicians had their own hangovers to deal with. Predictably, the mood in the halls of our universities (if my social media feeds are anything to go by) could be summed up in one word: nervous. When and where will the government hammer fall next?

Some of us worry about the embarrassingly uninformed commentary from Coalition politicians about research funding that appeared just before polling day. 'Useless' research was mocked and we academics were firmly put in our place: as icing on the Australian worker cake who should be grateful for what they deign to hand out to us. But my feeling is that this is a sideshow which politicians can ill afford to indulge themselves in, and for one reason.

China.

I was recently lucky enough to catch a lecture at ANU given by Professor Simon Marginson, just as he was heading out of the country to take up a position with the University of London. Marginson was kind enough to share the slide deck with the audience, as he wants this data to be shared widely. The message in Marginson's lecture was that we should start contrasting the attitude of our politicians with the mood in Asia, where the scale of investment in higher education is breathtaking.

In fact, it's the sheer ambition of Asian states' investment in higher education which is jaw-dropping to your average Australian academic. We are so accustomed to the 'do more with less' mentality of policymakers over the last 20 years or more that we wouldn't know ambitious policy if it smacked us in the face. I know it wasn't just me who was shocked, as I was live-tweeting the lecture and the response was huge. Here are some pocket statistics I shared on the night that got the most interest:

- Australia is just behind the UK and the US in our share of the overseas student market – equal to Germany and France and marginally above Canada. We are punching far above our weight.
- We don't have any universities in the Shanghai ARWU top 50, but we do have five in the top 100 and a further 14 in the top 500. We are doing comparatively well there too.
- Our gross national income per head in 2011 was US$43 170 compared to China at $8390 and we compare well to most other countries in the OECD. In other words, we are rich. We can afford to invest more.
- Yet Australia's level of investment in research and development as a proportion of GDP is lower than that of most OECD countries and compares

favourably only with countries such as Brazil and
Poland.

- Asia is starting to eat our lunch when it comes to
educational outcomes and academic output.
- China's school students top all PISA metrics on
student outcomes. We are number nine for reading
and ten for science, but not even in the top ten for
mathematics.
- Between 1995 and 2009, China increased the
number of published journal papers by 65 000,
while Australia increased by only 10 000.
- There has been what Marginson calls a 'rapid
improvement' in China and Asia, with authors
from the region climbing the most-cited list. From
2000 to 2010, in chemistry alone, China increased
citations by 10 per cent while US citations
decreased by over 14 per cent.

The audience couldn't help but draw one conclusion: compared to our timid politicians, Asian leaders
seem startlingly optimistic about higher education.
This optimism has been followed up with significant
investment in education at all levels, which is only
beginning to bear fruit. If the trends are going to be
anything to go by, Australia is heading in one direction: down. In fact, the recitation of these statistics
prompted a member of the audience to ask (with some

concern) if our grandchildren will want to go to China to get a 'quality education' because it would no longer be available at home. Marginson agreed this conclusion was unavoidable, but emphasised the positives of the 'reverse international student experience'.

I couldn't help reflecting on who would have access to this 'quality education' in the future, thinking of the international students of today. It won't be the majority of our middle class who get to study in top-flight Chinese institutions, let alone anyone else.

So I decided to stop being depressed about the lack of respect for higher education displayed by politicians and start being angry at the lack of investment, at the lack of ambition and the blatant pandering to the anti-elitist vote at the expense of our children and grandchildren. It's this anger that is going to be motivating my vote when I next walk down to get my #democracysausage.

💬 FAKE NOSTALGIA

To riff on a famous Douglas Adams quote: 'To academics, time is an illusion – and in the case of the due date for a book chapter, doubly so.'

Putting together an edited book is a relatively thankless task with a degree of difficulty of at least ten. Marshalling authors, hassling them to submit, editing, polishing, typesetting ... It's such a labour-intensive process that it's no wonder by the time the book actually arrives on your desk you may well not remember even writing the chapter you contributed.

Such is the case with *Through a Glass Darkly: The Social Sciences Look at the Neoliberal University*, a collection of essays put together by Margaret Thornton after an Academy of the Social Sciences Australia (ASSA) workshop on the 'marketisation of the university' held in 2013. I might not remember writing the chapter I contributed to it, but I do remember the workshop that led to the book. Some excellent papers were given about the state of universities today and what might happen in the future. A lot of the talk at the workshop turned on the changes in academia over the last 20 years: the increase in performance metrics, the push for academics to get more and more funding and the increasing casualisation of the academic workforce.

Themes that will no doubt be quite familiar to you.

In the book itself all this talk is distilled into sharp academic arguments and couched in sophisticated language – which is an interesting contrast with the event itself. What surprised me most about the day was how emotional it was, especially the reaction to one of the papers, which concerned a faculty torn apart by restructures. The author, with tears in her eyes, expressed her deep disillusionment with the university to whom she, and many others, had given so many years of loyal service. As the academic told her story, the grey heads around the table nodded in sympathy and started sharing similar stories. The grief around the table for academia lost was palpable.

Later, in the tearoom, I discussed the paper, and our older colleagues' reactions to it, with my fellow 40-somethings. We were all members of the so-called 'sessional generation' and we didn't quite know how we should feel about this outpouring of grief. Our older colleagues had memories of an academia we had only ever read about in books: the Australian university in the '50s, '60s and '70s which, so the story goes, was well funded and well respected by the government and community alike.

It's impossible to feel genuinely nostalgic about something you have never experienced. It was like being at a funeral for your friend's great-aunt; someone you'd heard a lot about, but never met in person. Your friend is grieving. You know you should be sad, but you can't really feel what they're feeling. So you just pat your friend awkwardly on the shoulder and say, 'Well, she had a good innings, didn't she?'

Those of us who have entered academia this century have learned that loyalty to an institution is something you can't afford to feel. The upside to this, if there is one, is not experiencing grief and loss when you leave. So far I've survived four restructures at three different universities. Maybe I'll be made redundant one day too. The prospect doesn't fill me with joy, but I'm not that afraid of it either, because I always have a back-up plan – that's just what the sessional generation has to do.

You see, the sessional generation has been bred to be self-interested. But working in your own best interest should not always be conflated with selfishness. This was the essence of my talk at the workshop and the chapter I helped write in the book. Sharing – a principle on which unionism is built – just makes sense. Sharing makes us stronger in the face of government self-interest and declining university budgets. For example, I give away my ideas via freely available slide decks, podcasts, cheat sheets, blog posts and the like. I lose nothing by sharing and I gain reputation – the only cultural currency an academic can use.

Self-interest means actively looking for opportunities to experience collegiality. Sadly, our universities pay our wages, but they don't really provide our academic home anymore. We have to build those for ourselves. I am grateful to be surrounded by many academic sisters and brothers doing it for themselves on Twitter. I actively look for role models there, people who know how to survive and thrive. My friend Megan is a stand-out inspiration in this respect. At the moment Megan mostly does research project management work, but she has taught casually for years, makes art, sells it and is in the process of finishing her PhD part-time. When I was in a similar situation, working casual jobs at three different universities and trying to do a research degree, I was completely demoralised. But where I saw only lemons, Megan sees lemonade.

She has even managed to get a mortgage from a bank. Degree of difficulty on that? On a scale of ten, it's an 11.

 THE ANGRY RANT, RECONSIDERED

My usual *Advocate* column writing strategy is to:

1   Work myself into a froth of rage about something.
2   Release the words.

As a consequence, my columns are really thinly disguised rants and I am grateful that the editors continue to publish them (thanks, Paul and Jenny). There was plenty to be angry about this month, but a post on *The Research Whisperer* called It Gets Worse, about the plight of the academic 'precariat', made me so crazy that I passed over some kind of anger event horizon and ended up feeling ... numb. Go and read it, but be warned: I spent most of the day lying on my office floor, feeling like the survivor of a plane crash and wondering what the hell I was doing with my life.

Here's the thing: I get plenty of positive reader responses from angry rants. No one writes to me when I publish a happy piece, either here or on my blog. I started to wonder, if we are so angry, why do we keep going to work? In an effort to explore this topic I took note of all the things I enjoyed about working in academia this week and came up with a starter list for you:

- Campus gardens: all week I admired them, yet I never saw anyone doing any actual gardening. Is there a secret army of university house elves that tirelessly labour at night to make such delightful topiary outside building 144? It's a mystery.
- Lunchrooms – even the one in my building, which is full of passive-aggressive notes about cleaning up and demands for money, either for lollies or teabags.
- Colleagues' bookshelves – the best are works of art, diligently compiled over decades. The well-composed academic bookshelf should quietly intimidate, while exuding an air of effortlessly confident intellectual superiority. I keep a serious book on orgies in mine, just to confuse people.
- Cold, bitter coffee – the sort that is only found at conferences. I can drink it by the bucketload. It's honestly better cold – heating it up only makes it worse.
- What passes for 'fashion' in committee meetings – look closely at everyone's shoes next time you're bored and you'll see what I mean.
- Academic door decorations – someone once stuck a post-it note on my friend Emily Kothe's door saying: 'Ask me about my [overdue task]', so that everyone would nag her about it. Apparently it worked.

Curious as to what others thought of my list, I posted it on social media. The comments confirmed that I am not the only person to enjoy the oddities of academic life.

My friend Kim Barbour enjoys seeing students reading in weird places, 'like the broken chair in a stairwell'. She also takes pleasure in 'Stationery cupboards, including the second-hand bits, old cassette tapes, and weird bits of plastic that no one remembers the purpose of'. Lyndon Walker agreed and noted that campuses are one of the few places you are likely to encounter working VCR players.

But Lyndon saves his love for old buildings 'with corridors that go nowhere'. Campus buildings really are a constant source of fascination and delight. Susan Mayson noted the power of empty corridors where 'you know everyone is working … somewhere'. Joyce Seitzinger pointed out that library spaces are especially great. Lyndon likes old library books and I'll admit I get a bit of a kick out of the smell of old paper. Is it mould? I'm not sure.

The neglected stuff on campus does exert a powerful fascination. On Twitter @katja_Thieme admitted that she enjoyed 'finding and collecting the nice pens and pencils that others have left behind in class and seminar rooms'. My friend Tseen Khoo even started a Tumblr blog, *Sad Chairs of Academia*, to celebrate the forgotten and unloved chairs on university campuses. My PhD student Jodie-Lee Trembath reminisced about an office chair that was 'so decrepit that I wrapped black plastic around the cushions then covered the plastic in blankets and scarves so I wouldn't get mites when I sat in it'.

Jodie also pointed out 'The hilarious, hyper intelligent debates people get into via graffiti on the back of toilet doors'. Personally, I've been enjoying those since about 1989.

Campus wildlife got rave reviews from my academic friends and followers. Rachael Pitt likes ducks, and other critters such as cats, turtles, rabbits and water dragons got special mentions. ANU has a fine collection of kangaroos on our coastal campus. There was a certain 'Professor Roo' who used to hang out on the lawn in front of the ANU Law School a couple of years ago. During our induction events the international students were warned to keep their distance because Professor Roo could be a bit, well, grumpy. My friend Xan Hordern pointed out that some of the human wildlife can be a bit grumpy too, but there are wonderful elderly academics to be found on every campus. We agreed that the best kind wore knitted cardies, or sandals with socks. Student politics are a curiosity too, aren't they? Charlotte Pezaro likes seeing the Socialist Alliance with their clipboards and I love signing their petitions. There's always an atmosphere of earnest flirtation between all those bright young things sharing their political passions. I'm sure many a marriage starts there.

I could go on and on, but now I'm 100 words over my limit (sorry, Paul). I'm glad I made and shared my list. After spending a couple of hours reflecting and compiling this list of things to love about academia, I felt a lot better about life.

I hope you do too.

💬 VALE, GOUGH WHITLAM (A TRIBUTE, IN FOUR PARTS)

Sometime early in 1975. Monash University forecourt. Market day.

I am four and a half years old. My mother has my twin sister and me by the hand as we walk through an enormous plaza surrounded by towering square buildings. The wind whips my short skirt up above my waist and flings building site dust in my face. I'm confused, tired and want to go to the toilet. I start crying and sit on the ground, refusing to move any further. My sister stops to look at a bug, uninterested in my hysterics, while my mother bends down to wipe my face. I ask her when we are going home. She tells me we are at a university, an important place, and that one day, years from now, I will come here to learn things. She told me that, even though I had a lot of school to go yet, she was sure I was going to university because a man called Gough Whitlam had changed things so kids like me had a chance.

———————

Late 1975. The family lounge room, inside a modest, triple-fronted brick veneer in the suburbs.

My mother is standing by the television, crying. My father is standing, stony-faced, with his arm around her. I'm deeply confused. I ask them what is wrong and they don't answer. I lean around them to see what is on the television. There's a black and white image of a whole lot of men standing on some white steps. I recognise Gough Whitlam from the newspaper my father reads in the mornings. He's giving a speech. Now I know that what he said was 'Well may we say God save the Queen, because nothing will save the Governor-General' because I have it on a mug in my office, but at the time I only saw that he was angry. 'What will happen to our girls?' my mother asks my father tearfully. He just looks at her, sadly.

———————

Sometime in 1990. The steps of the Victorian Parliament House.

I'm 19 and I've just started university. My mother has cancer. The house in the suburbs is sold. There's no room for me there, even if I wanted to move back. I barely understand this new thing called the Higher Education Contribution Scheme that I've signed up to. It seems so complicated, but I'm grateful I can pay for my tertiary education through my taxes later. I don't have to find money upfront for university fees so I can still fulfil my ambition of getting an architecture degree. I'm living on Austudy and around $120 a week from working in a bookstore. I'm poor, which is not helped by the fact that I have taken up both drinking and smoking, much to my mother's disgust. She worries I won't finish my degree, but her worry is unnecessary. University is amazing, scary, harder than I ever thought possible. I'm hooked on learning, even if my grades are reflecting the amount of time I'm spending smoking and drinking with my new musician friends.

I'm here today, on these steps, because the government is talking about cutting Austudy. I'm really worried that I won't be able to pay the rent for my mouse-infested share house. A recession has just hit and people aren't buying books. My hours at the bookstore have been cut. So I'm protesting with my sister and a few friends. Again. Colleen holds up a sign saying that the education minister is the new Sheriff of Nottingham. 'Where is Gough?' asks another sign, plaintively.

Suddenly I'm caught up in a mass of students, rushing towards the front windows of Parliament House. I hear glass breaking and then mounted police arrive. Those horses are scary when you're under their hooves. I actually have a moment where I think I'm going to die and I break away from the crowd. I make it to a quiet side street. I wonder where my sister and my friends are as I light a cigarette with shaking hands. Smoking calms me and I get to thinking. These protests will gain nothing. It's the Labor Party who is stiffing us this time. I realise something profound: the government doesn't care about me.

―――――――

It's 2009. The stage in the Conservatorium at the University of Melbourne.

A man in a floppy hat is talking and I am standing on the side of the stage in academic robes. I've got the same floppy hat as the Chancellor. The hat has been worn by so many people before me that the brim has taken on an odd shape. It won't sit on my head properly.

My name is called and I walk carefully across the stage to take the roll of paper from the man's hands. He smiles and shakes my hand, saying something I barely hear as I search the crowd for familiar faces. My husband, sister, father and son smile at me and applaud loudly. It's a good day. I am finally a doctor. There is no more university to do. Suddenly I remember that day in the Monash University plaza and my mother's words. She has been dead now for nearly a decade. She would be amazed that this university thing has gone as far as it has. I'm sad she's not here. She would have so enjoyed bragging to her friends. I send her a silent thank you.

And I add in another silent thanks, to Gough.

REFERENCES

Allen, D. (2002). *How to get things done: the art of stress-free productivity*. Ringwood, Vic.: Penguin.

Becker, H. S. (2007). *Writing for social scientists: how to start and finish your thesis, book or article*. Chicago: University of Chicago Press.

Booker, C. (2004). *The seven basic plots: why we tell stories*. London: Continuum.

Burt, R. S. (2002). 'Social origins of good ideas.' Discussion paper, University of Chicago and the Raytheon Company, <www.analytictech.com/mb709/readings/burt_SOGI.pdf>

Denholm, C. J. and Evans, T. D. (2012). *Doctorates downunder: keys to successful doctoral study in Australia and Aotearoa New Zealand*. Camberwell, Vic.: ACER Press.

Hartley, J. (2007). 'There's more to the title than meets the eye: exploring the possibilities', *Technical Writing and Communication*, 37(1), 95–101.

Johnson, S. (2011). *Where good ideas come from: the natural history of innovation*. New York: Riverhead Books.

Kamler, B. and Thomson, P. (2014). *Helping doctoral students write: pedagogies for supervision*. London: Routledge.

Kiley, M. and Wisker, G. (2009). 'Threshold concepts in research education and evidence of threshold crossing'. *Higher Education Research & Development*, 28(4), 431–441. <doi.org/10.1080/07294360903067930>

Kondo, M. (2014). *The life-changing magic of tidying up: the Japanese art of decluttering and organizing*. Berkeley: Ten Speed Press.

Lamont, M. (2010). *How professors think: inside the curious world of academic judgment*. Cambridge, MA: Harvard University Press.

Lamott, A. (2008). *Bird by bird: some instructions on writing and life*. Melbourne: Scribe.

Newport, C. (2012). *So good they can't ignore you: why skills trump passion in the quest for work you love.* New York: Grand Central Publishing.

Phillips, E., Pugh, D. S. and Johnson, C. (2015). *How to get a PhD: a handbook for students and their supervisors.* Maidenhead, UK: Open University Press.

Petre, M. and Rugg, G. (2010). *The unwritten rules of PhD research.* Maidenhead, UK: Open University Press.

Pitt, R. and Mewburn, I. (2016). 'Academic superheroes? A critical analysis of academic job descriptions'. *Journal of Higher Education Policy and Management*, 38(1), 88. <doi.org/10.1080/136008 0X.2015.1126896>

Schneider, A. 'Frumpy or chic? Tweed or kente? Sometimes clothes make the professor', *Chronicle of Higher Education*, 23 January 1998, <www. chronicle.com/article/Frumpy-or-Chic-Tweed-or/65194>

Sutton, R. I. (2010). *The no asshole rule: building a civilized workplace and surviving one that isn't.* New York: Business Plus.

Thornton, M., ed. (2014). *Through a Glass Darkly.* Canberra: ANU Press.

Ward, M. (2013). 'Living in liminal space: the PhD as accidental pedagogy'. Unpublished doctoral dissertation. University of Sydney.

White, B. (2011). *Mapping your thesis: the comprehensive manual of theory and techniques for masters and doctoral research.* Melbourne: ACER Press.

BLOGS

The Research Whisperer: https://theresearchwhisperer.wordpress.com
The Brown Car Blog: browncar.tumblr.com
Patter: https://patthomson.net
Research Degree Voodoo: https://researchvoodoo.wordpress.com
Pretentious Title: thisblogisaploy.blogspot.com.au
Explorations in Style: https://explorationsofstyle.com
Campus Morning Mail: campusmorningmail.com.au

INDEX

316

Index

Index

Index

Index